In his galvanizing book *Embracing the New*  *Our Multiethnic Future*, Dr. Alex Mandes e____ work in the harvest fields of what he calls S____ multiethnic America. He powerfully weave____ to flesh out how God consistently transforms p____ ____ ____ self-preservation into a diverse, unified, and missional community. Readers will be challenged and convicted—but also ex____ ____ ____ in on what God is doing in our neighborhoods around the world. A must-read for any who wonder what God has been up to lately.

> WALTER KIM, president of the National Association of Evangelicals

Embracing the New Samaria is a Gospel-centered, transformational invitation to see differently. Alex calls us beyond myopic, homogeneous visions of the Kingdom of God to a glorious multiethnic revival rooted in the *missio Christi* which embraces the modern-day Samarias beyond preference, privilege, or prejudice. It is a journey the church in America should boldly embrace anew.

> REV. DR. GABRIEL SALGUERO, pastor at The Gathering Place, president of the National Latino Evangelical Coalition

In *Embracing the New Samaria*, Dr. Mandes casts a vision for the body of Christ to hold the Great Commission and Great Commandment in a healthy tension by intentionally leaning into disciplemaking inclusive of justice and compassion, yielding a transformed community of believers. The prophetic instruction applies to a broad swarth of believers: those curious about engaging the "other" in their communities, those with firmly held convictions of God's call into the uncomfortable, unfamiliar, and those currently engaged and seeking an alternative viewpoint. *Embracing the New Samaria* is a call for Christians to open their hearts to the humbling work of pursuing biblical justice, racial reconciliation, and the diversity of God's Kingdom. And to open their eyes, see the opportunities around them, and offer strategic next steps toward living on earth as it is in heaven.

> APRIL WARFIELD, director of multicultural ministries for the Evangelical Free Church in America

In the Gospel of Luke, the disciple John eagerly suggests calling down fire on a village of the geographically proximate but ethnically and religiously different Samaritans, a suggestion Jesus firmly rebukes. Apparently John eventually learned to emulate Jesus' love for those on the margins because in the book of Acts, John prays for the Samaritans to receive the Holy Spirit. In *Embracing the New Samaria*, my friend Dr. Alejandro Mandes challenges and exhorts the church to follow Jesus' call to love, seek justice for, disciple, and be discipled by those on the margins of our society. I pray that many will read this engaging, biblically rooted book and, like John, embrace the vision of Christ's beautifully multiethnic Kingdom.

> **MATTHEW SOERENS**, US director of church mobilization and advocacy at World Relief

This is a book long overdue from one of evangelicalism's most ardent, credible, and proven champions of equitable inclusion of the marginalized in the full life and expression of the local church. My good friend and colleague, Dr. Alejandro Mandes, herein provides a personal, pastoral, and practical guide for twenty-first-century ministry leaders determined to advance a credible witness by establishing churches that embody the good news of God's love and hope for all people—not just some—in an increasingly diverse society. To get beyond rhetoric to results in this regard, I commend to you this work and encourage a passionate pursuit of its aim.

> **DR. MARK DEYMAZ**, founding pastor/directional leader of Mosaic Church of Central Arkansas, cofounder and president of Mosaix Global Network, author of *Building a Healthy Multi-ethnic Church* and *The Coming Revolution in Church Economics*

In *Embracing the New Samaria*, Alex Mandes gives a clarion call for us to see our communities through the eyes of missionaries. For the church to effectively live out the Lord's mission, we must intentionally look for the unreached, the unengaged, and the unnoticed people around us and then consider how we can effectively share with them the good news of the gospel in both word and deed. As we do, the Lord will be glorified through the multiplication of transformational churches among all people!

> **KEVIN KOMPELIEN**, president of EFCA

Amid the great demographic shifts happening before our eyes, Dr. Mandes gives us a nuanced take on what it means to make disciples among a diverse group of people to build what he calls the *Great Community*. This book will help both majority- and minority-culture leaders reimagine who is in their Samaria and how to make disciples more effectively among them.

DANIEL YANG, director of the Send Institute

I love this gift Alex is bringing to the body of Christ in the form of *Embracing the New Samaria*. Alex's vision of a future that will more fully reflect God's intended design (Revelation 7:9) and of the opportunity we have to live and see the Kingdom of God manifest through his people is compelling and challenging. I commit to Alex's call for us to move forward as learners, with the humility of Christ, to ask the Lord to open our eyes as his people, so we can join him in seeing this beautiful, multicolored, multicultural tapestry come into being. The future and fate of the church depends on it.

DOUG NUENKE, US president of The Navigators

In this penetrating and challenging book, Alex Mandes shows us how to appreciate what a special gift those who are different from us racially or culturally are. Alex's book is the fruit of a lifetime of living and ministering as a "minority in a majority world." This book has literally opened my eyes to the many ways I've looked past my dear neighbors like Alex and have therefore not only done them deep disservice but also missed out on the treasure that they would have been to me if I could've only seen them and allowed them to come alongside of me in my daily life and ministry. His book is not only about ministering *to* "Samerica," as he calls it, but being blessed to minister *with* our brothers and sisters of different races and cultures. If you're looking for a caustic and judgmental blast at most of us, you'll not find it here. Instead, what Alex provides is a winsome, but provocative, challenge of our preferences and prejudices—and an invitation to the many possibilities of a far more beautiful, fruitful life and ministry through living and working alongside those we might have previously overlooked or even looked down on.

DAVID V. MARTIN, DD, director of EDA Move for GATEWAY Theological Institute

Mandes calls majority-culture Christians and churches to engage the new Samaria that is this country. Passionate, practical, informed by personal experience, and grounded in biblical texts, this work exhorts its readers to embrace "orthodance," the confluence of orthodoxy and orthopraxy. The American church needs to revitalize its mission by doing compassionate justice, making disciples, planting multiethnic churches, and providing relevant leadership training. A timely word by an eminent practitioner!

DANIEL CARROLL, Scripture Press Ministries professor of biblical studies and pedagogy, Wheaton College

Alex Mandes is a visionary leader helping churches minister to immigrants. He has instilled the passion and provided the tools to do so in his own denomination, where he serves as executive director of ethnic, immigrant, and justice programs. And he's built effective, replicable systems now used by many churches outside his denomination. In this book, Alex clearly explains why the Great Commission requires that we make disciples beyond those who are "just like us." And—most importantly—he provides specifics on how to do so. It's an easy, insightful read for church leaders and a great resource for small groups and individuals who want to reach their neighbors in the margins and fulfill the Great Commission.

LARRY ROBERTS, chief operating officer (ret.) of the Free Methodist Church—USA

An excellent book from Dr. Alex Mandes! In this deeply personal, transparent book, he causes us (in a healthy way) to stop, think, examine, and see things differently, to gain a better glimpse of God's perspective concerning the diverse communities that make up America. Mandes helps the reader understand how God wants to use us and his church to reach the people surrounding us. You will be far richer for having read this book!

BOB ROWLEY, superintendent of EFCA Texas–Oklahoma

Embracing the new Samaria

Opening Our Eyes to Our Multiethnic Future

ALEJANDRO MANDES

With Deborah Sáenz Gonzalez

A NavPress resource published in alliance
with Tyndale House Publishers

NavPress is the publishing ministry of The Navigators, an international Christian organization and leader in personal spiritual development. NavPress is committed to helping people grow spiritually and enjoy lives of meaning and hope through personal and group resources that are biblically rooted, culturally relevant, and highly practical.

For more information, visit NavPress.com.

27 26 25 24 23 22 21
7   6   5   4   3   2   1

To my dear mentor William J. Hamel, now with the Lord. He told me what I needed to hear whether I wanted to hear it or not. He was rarely wrong. I won't hold being a Packer fan against him. He made me a better minister of the gospel. He knew what sacrificial compassion and justice for the oppressed meant and worked to see it happen.

To my faithful friend and wife Julie Ann Mandes (Strand from North Dakota). She discipled and continues to disciple our five daughters: Sonia, Amanda, Joanna, Katie, and Emily. People said we should not wed: "Hispanic fire and Nordic ice don't go together." Our relationship of diverse diversity proves the thesis of the book. Diversity can offer vistas and hope to see heaven on earth now when lived out in love and the power of the Holy Spirit. Putting a jalapeño in her cranberry relish is just the tip of the iceberg.

CONTENTS

FOREWORD

IN JANUARY 2010, I went to speak at a gathering in Phoenix to bring attention to the humiliating way immigrants were being treated by the authorities. They were being housed in tents in the desert and dressed in pink. It was intended to be humiliating. For me, those were men made in the image of God. I loved and cared for them as if they were my brothers. It was not a funny matter.

Many may have wondered what an African American Bible teacher and civil rights worker was doing in Phoenix caring about Latin American men being toyed with for the amusement of the legal authorities detaining them—people using their power to humiliate because they could. The plight of these immigrants took me back to a similar time in my life where people would abuse their authority because they could.

In Phoenix I wasn't looking for a platform for myself. I was there to help the evangelical church wake up. An evangelical myself, I had a right to speak to them, to help them understand that we are all one family—one people, one church, and one faith.

We need to love one another. If my brown family suffers, I suffer. All that we learned in the civil rights struggle is not just for black people. We are *one* people. Unbeknown to me, my son Alex Mandes told me later, those words were fresh water on his head.

He had never heard a Bible teacher speak of justice for all people. Those words of concern from a black man drove home the point that we are one family. Since then the relationship between myself and Alex has grown in many ways outside of the view of many.

In 2018, Alex encouraged me to speak at a conference in San Antonio on justice and the gospel. I agreed to the opportunity under one condition: that he spend one extra day just with me, walking me through the Alamo and the history of the immigrant experience.

As we walked through the city, we discovered our similar spiritual formation and values rooted in the Word and for discipleship, which ran even deeper than our color and cultural differences. We both share the deep desire to tear down walls of division. We see justice and reconciliation as only possible for a committed disciple of the Lord Jesus Christ. We share the commitment to elevate love for our neighbor as the greatest commandment (Galatians 5:14).

We also shared many pains and disappointments together. Our greatest lament was the church's inability to see that our God-given differences of diversity are a gift. That gift of diversity is given to reach the whole world; diversity is not something to divide us. Diversity is not even the objective in life. But if we can't learn to love people different than ourselves, then the main objective, bringing the whole world to him, will never be accomplished.

As we walked and talked over meals in San Antonio, Alex shared a desire to write a book. At that time, I encouraged my son to write what was on our hearts. I promised to write the foreword. During the pandemic, I called him and gave him some advice but added a stiff emphasis on the urgency in light of these present days of unrest, division, and the loss of Christlike love. Alex, like an obedient son, completed the book we had talked about in 2018.

For us, reconciliation includes walking out justice and compassion as a part of making disciples. The fruit of that true reconciliation is that the church will grow. That fruit will remain, and that fruit will give itself to God, as it was produced by God. The result of the fruit is those lives surrendered to Christ in a walk of discipleship living such that the people around the church, even if not believers in Christ, will know that there is a God because of our love.

I hear in Alex's message the same message God has given me, that love is the greatest fruit of the Spirit. It is all, in all, over all— the greatest expression of God, the greatest gift of God.

With a full heart I recommend this work—a different accent between us on how to say things but the prophetic call is clearly the same. I am proud to add this son, this book to the Perkins library of kindred spirits.

John M. Perkins

INTRODUCTION

MARTIN LUTHER KING JR. had a dream—one that he so eloquently delivered on August 28, 1963: a hope for freedom, equality, and justice in the United States. Almost sixty years later, I also have a dream—my *sueño*—that I will spend my life's work trying to achieve. My *sueño* is to someday see all people living together in unity here on earth as it is in heaven.

Two biblical passages ground my dream in prophetic reality. One is the vision of all people around the throne of God described in Revelation 7. It reads:

> After these things I looked, and behold, a great multitude which no one could number, of all nations, tribes, peoples, and tongues, standing before the throne and before the Lamb, clothed with white robes, with palm branches in their hands, and crying out with a loud voice, saying, "Salvation belongs to our God who sits on the throne, and to the Lamb!"
>
> REVELATION 7:9-10

This is a prophetic view of what the Kingdom of God will be like—with all nations, tribes, peoples, and tongues worshiping God together around his throne. What a heavenly vision! The other biblical passage that grips me is from Matthew 6, when Jesus teaches his disciples how to pray. He gave us these words:

> Our Father in heaven,
> Hallowed be Your name.
> Your kingdom come.
> Your will be done
> On earth as it is in heaven.
> MATTHEW 6:9-10

When we pray these words, we are asking God to help us live out his heavenly vision *now*—alongside people of all nations, tribes, and tongues—not just when we die and join him in his presence, but here on earth, today.

How We've Missed the Mark

Disappointingly, some of our churches and ministries do not reflect the earthly prayer that God prophetically laid out for us in the Scriptures. When we envision "making disciples" in our local contexts, we tend to think about reaching people who are just like us, and our churches tend to reflect that reality. In the United States, 86 percent of Protestant congregations are made up of one predominant racial group, making Sunday mornings one of the most segregated times of the week. Even more telling is that 53 percent of churchgoers think their church is diverse enough.[1]

It is painfully obvious that we have failed to see, love, and reach our neighbors who are different from us. Furthermore, many of us have made peace with tepid complacency, believing that this is as good as it can get. Some of us compensate for such saltless obedience with man-made panache, "excellence," bling, and beautiful branding, but the fact remains that a mediocre approach to disciplemaking is not getting us to the Kingdom vision of Revelation 7. It is killing us. We miss the true transformation that awaits us. Let God be God! We can't out-wow God!

Brothers and sisters, I do not believe that God called us to do something that can't be done. I do believe we can have heaven on earth. I am not speaking of a future dispensation. My hope and dream is that we fully realize the Lord's visionary prayer now. What we see now in the form of national ethnic and immigrant tensions does not have to define our future. It doesn't have to be that way.

In this book I will have fun exploring the fictitious life of Ebenezer Scrooge, who lived a dreary life of selfishness. Three ghosts assist him to see how he has lived a wasted life of selfishness. The final ghost, the ghost of Christmas future, ends by showing Scrooge the results of his selfish, lonely life. Scrooge, now fully grasping the missed opportunity of doing good to his fellow man, asks the third ghost if the things that were shown to him are the things that must be, or might be if he doesn't repent. This is the point where Scrooge wakes up from his night visions.

Dear ones, it is not too late for us to live transformed lives. I call for us to walk the walk of God with our eyes wide open. Mankind is our business! The Holy Spirit will give us the power. May my call to the GC3 (Great Commandment, Great Commission, and Great Community) be as effective as Ebenezer's three spirits in rousing us to see that we should live every day doing good to all mankind! Maranatha!

Who This Book Is For

I wrote this book to help my evangelical[2] family—specifically those who are part of the majority culture—to transcend the status quo by loving and reaching their neighbors in the margins, as God has called us to do.

Some might read the term *majority culture* and wonder why I'm not just using the term *white*, since in the United States generally this is true. But I grew up in Laredo, Texas, a city along the US-Mexico border that is majority Hispanic, so even though I am an ethnic minority in the United States, I grew up in the majority culture for my local context. And even there, in a border town that exists in the margins of American society, I've witnessed vulnerable people of various ethnicities experiencing marginalization at the hands of their own ethnic groups. So depending on where you live, the majority culture may or may not be white—but one thing is for sure: Our sinful natures make us all capable of judging people unworthy and excluding or ignoring them as a consequence.

Some of you may have picked up this book because you sense that the church needs to change but you are unsure where to start. Others may already be taking steps outside of your comfort zone but want to know how to take it to the next level. Then, of course, some readers may be further along in the journey and interested in hearing a new perspective. I am incredibly grateful for the Christians who have worked hard to embody biblical justice, racial reconciliation, and the diversity of God's Kingdom here on earth. They are wonderful examples for us all—but there is never an end point. We all have work to do, and the purpose of this book is to be a brotherly prophetic call for us all to open our eyes, acknowledge the divine opportunity that is in front of us, and start taking steps toward the dream. I hope that my perspective as a bicultural (Mexican and American) person who has lived and worked in both majority-culture and marginal spaces will help guide us through the challenges and opportunities we face as a multiethnic body of Christ.

How did we get to the point of ignoring disciplemaking in the margins? I believe some of us have been so focused on either the Great Commission (spreading the Good News to the ends of the earth) *or* the Great Commandment (loving your neighbor as yourself) that we have failed to see the inextricable connection between the two, which when lived out together results in a Great Transformed Community of believers. I call this the GC3:

THE GREAT COMMISSION AND GREAT COMMANDMENT BUILD GREAT COMMUNITY.

Many Christian churches and parachurches have given more emphasis to either the love mandate or the disciplemaking mandate, so that energy spent on one seems to take away from the other. Few have been good at holding both in a healthy tension. You can find lots of books on disciplemaking and church planting, and you can find lots of books on justice and compassion, but you won't find many books that systematically and intentionally join those two great themes together. These four ideas are connected, however: Love/justice and disciplemaking/church planting combine to bring transformation in our communities. This is the essence of the GC3, which I will share more about in chapter 7 and refer to throughout the book.

When I see the ministry of Jesus, I see people being discipled and matters of compassion and justice being addressed fluidly. I don't see Jesus wearing his justice hat one day and his disciplemaker hat the next. I see transformation at all levels. If we want a Great Community—a transformed church helping to transform the surrounding community who are not yet Christ followers—we must commit ourselves to both the Great Commission and the Great Commandment.

Life in the Margins

I was born to see life in the margins. Raised in Laredo, Texas, a city on the Texas-Mexico border, I grew up quite literally in the margins of this country. My mother's family has lived in this region for generations, even before it was part of the United States. It surprises some people to hear that my ancestors didn't "come to this country," especially those who are not familiar with the history of the Southwest region of the United States. As the saying goes, "We didn't cross the border; the border crossed us." My parents and I were not immigrants, but if we had been born just a few miles south of where we were, our story would be very different.

When I lived in Laredo, the population was about seventy thousand people, the majority of whom were of Mexican descent, Mexican immigrants, or "Tejanos." The people I grew up around spoke English, Spanish, and Spanglish (a mixture of English and Spanish that has become its own language of sorts). The closest big city, San Antonio, is 150 miles away, making Laredo, like few cities in America, an isolated bubble with its own unique culture, language, and set of rules. While there is a border/bridge dividing Laredo and its Mexican sister city, Nuevo Laredo, the border was not a barrier. People have family on both sides and, at least in those years, crossed easily and frequently. (The key enforcement on immigration takes place at the Border Patrol station twenty miles outside of the city, so we didn't even need passports to cross between the border cities.) Gas, medicine, and tortillas were always cheaper in Mexico. Garments, gadgets, and work opportunities were always better on the Texas side. When I was young, and my friends and I wanted to play hooky from school, we would pay a nickel at the bridge and go to the theater across the border, with no worries at all that the truant officer would bother us in Mexico.

Of the largest five hundred cities in America, Laredo is at the bottom of the list in terms of cultural and ethnic diversity, coming in at number 489.[3] I tell people that when I was young I knew there were white and black people in America because I saw them on TV. Growing up in a minority-majority, mostly Spanish-speaking, monocultural city, let's just say I did not have the typical ethnic minority experience.

One might wonder how I came to be so passionate about diversity and reaching people who are different than me given such a monocultural upbringing. If there was ever something that is of God, it is this. Through my faith journey, God has bestowed upon me an immense love for all people, but especially those in the margins. And I have spent my entire adult life sharing my passions and convictions while navigating through white evangelical spaces. Though it has been challenging, I have welcomed the adventure because it is where my calling lies.

My Spiritual Conversion

It all began when I put my faith in Christ in high school. When I was a young boy, my family was Catholic. I remember attending a Catholic retreat and developing a strong interest in spiritual things. They helped me ask the right questions, but the problem was they didn't help me find the answers. The Catholic church has come a long way since Vatican II, but back in the 1970s I had a hard time growing spiritually in my local church context. Their greatest gift to me was a Bible at the end of the retreat. I read that Bible cover to cover and knew there was something there, but I couldn't quite figure out how to take it to the next level.

In the summer of 1973, a man named Carlos Cuellar finished his education and boot camp and was stationed at the Laredo Air Force Base, where he joined a Bible study led by Captain Gary Combs. Carlos and I had a mutual friend named Angela, who started attending the Bible study and was led to the Lord. Angela then introduced me to Captain Combs, and I never turned back.

I put my faith in Christ and started walking to the Air Force base every week to be in their Bible study. A man named Pancho Garcia began discipling me, and his fiancée, Lilia Vasquez, also played a crucial role in nurturing my walk with the Lord. I was so blessed to be around committed disciples in Laredo. I can't tell my story without mentioning them and the deep value for disciplemaking I've had from the very beginning of my spiritual life. I could not get enough of it, and these dear souls gave time to a lowly high school student who was very needy.

My life was marked by major transformation. I went everywhere with my big black New American Standard Bible and my big wooden cross necklace. Bathroom, band hall, *everywhere*. I wouldn't lay that Bible down without putting a white cloth under it. I was a real, stinking Jesus freak. Many of my high school friends said, "Leave Alex alone; he's going through a phase." But I did not want this to be a phase. So I made a pact with Jesus: I prayed that he would not leave me and that he would take my life before I would ever leave him. I made a commitment that *nothing* would stop me from being a disciple of Jesus Christ.

I didn't know what my spiritual gift was at the time, but one thing I knew for sure was that all of a sudden I had an immense love for people. I was never a very good student before my conversion, but after my conversion I had a huge hunger to read the Bible and to learn—not so much for my sake, but to be able to share with other people.

Never did I imagine that this love for all people would take me away from my family and my cocoon of a city. But in the mid-1970s the US government decided to close the Laredo Air Force Base, so the Bible study I had been attending—which was part of a ministry called The Navigators—would be ending. I was distraught. But the leaders told me if I wanted to continue to be discipled by The Navigators ministry, I could go to the University of Texas in Austin, and they would be there. Without knowing what that meant or how painful it would be, off I went.

Off to "Gringolandia"

Not only was I the first person in my family to go to college, but I was also the first of my siblings to leave Laredo, Texas. It was certainly disconcerting. On the day I packed up to move to Austin, I stood on the porch and received my mother's benediction, the sign of the cross, and she gave me her parting words of advice: "Stay away from the hippies."

When I arrived at the University of Texas in Austin, I was in full-bore culture shock for two weeks. It was only 240 miles away, but it might as well have been the other side of the earth. For the first time in my life, I felt like a minority. Everyone around me was white. There were drugs everywhere to be had. The feminist movement was in full swing, and women were being called to burn their bras. My mother's benediction and admonition to stay away from the hippies left me ill-prepared.

Eventually I developed friendships, but the culture continued to grate on my nature. To many of my friends, I was an enigma. I'd like to think I was an enjoyable enigma, but frankly, I was a little bit of a pain in the neck. I was one of about five people of color involved in campus ministry. My mates certainly were not offensive—they were kind—but it was clear from the beginning that I would need to adapt to their culture, and I did not fold that easily. I was okay with being a bit strange and very persistent, always offering a different perspective on things.

To be fair, looking back I realize that these were all young leaders like myself who were doing the best they could with what they knew. Fortunately, I had the kind of personality and mindset that nothing was going to turn me away, despite how painful it was at times. However, I'm certain there are many other non-majority-culture disciples who could not survive the predominately white Christian environment—both in those days and today—and they shouldn't have to. That reality speaks volumes about what needs to change. I will forever be grateful for the friends whom God sent to nurture my soul for him.

It is because of the marginal life I was born into—combined with my experience in highly impactful cross-cultural disciple-making/church planting, degrees in social work/community development, and theological training—that I have a deep passion to see God's church ready to reach the vulnerable and the marginalized. My concern for these brothers and sisters may seem sentimental to some, but it is in fact biblical and urgent: Western Christianity has pushed underrepresented and disadvantaged minority groups to the margins of its concern, in a similar way to how the people of God in the first century sent a whole people group to the fringes of the faith.

The New Samaria

In Acts 1:8, Jesus says to his disciples, "And you shall be witnesses to Me in Jerusalem, and in all Judea and Samaria, and to the end of the earth." Historically, Christians have taken this command to heart and flown missionaries all over the earth to spread the Good News. Today, however, we are living in a moment in history when Samaria and the ends of the earth have come to *us*. We are living in the New Samaria.

I often use the term *Samerica* to describe America, because I believe Samaria is here, all around us. This is true all around the world. Societies all over the globe have become increasingly diverse, multicultural, and multilingual. In North America, the Send Institute calls these areas global gateway cities.[4]

It is easy to miss the fact that the American immigration political conundrum is actually a global diaspora phenomenon. It is accelerating because of population growth and people's ability to move. No matter where you live, it's likely that people from every tribe, nation, and tongue are living in your neighborhoods, attending your schools, working hard to keep the economy running. Here in the United States, the children of immigrants are being born and raised here and will account for much of our nation's growth in the next fifty years. But this book is about more than just immigrants. It is about all of those who have been marginalized, ignored, and treated unjustly. The structures in our society have made it difficult for them to thrive, sometimes rendering them invisible. Unfortunately, it is no different inside the church. While some authors have written about the importance of having an evangelistic strategy for reaching the diaspora,[5] unfortunately much of the conversation remains at the academic level. Generally speaking, many Christians look at "outsiders" with sympathy but little relevant missional draw. And some Christians do see them, but their hands are so full with church programs that they can't engage. What I refer to as "the New Samaria"—or the "Samaritans" living among us—are the people who are near but different, the people we are literally flying over in order to fulfill the letter of a Great Commission to reach the ends of the earth.

Walking toward the Barking Dog

Even though Jesus' entire ministry was among those living life in the margins, somewhere along the way the vision of that got lost to the church. The disciples resisted seeing his passion for the marginalized, and today we are no different than the disciples, who saw little need for reaching the Samaritans of their day.

I often compare the demographic changes happening around us to a barking dog: The noise annoys us, so we move away from it. Similarly, many evangelicals shrink when faced with the barking dog of demographic shifts happening right under our noses. It is too complex a development for us, and we ignore it because we don't know what to do with it.

Frankly, I think the demographic shift is a barking dog that we must walk straight toward, and if we ignore it or put it off for someone else, we are missing out on its transformative power. From my perspective, the people in the margins are the blessing we must embrace as if our spiritual house depends on it. In fact, it does. We have become the New Samaria, and we must not look away. If we can get our spiritual mind around this, we will not only save the most vulnerable among us, we will save the church, ushering in the justice revival of Isaiah 58 that will give America another generation of life.

My Goal for This Book

My goal for this book is to help Christian leaders learn to *see, love, reach,* and ultimately *be* the New Samaria in a way that brings true transformation to our churches and communities. But in order to begin we need religious and cultural humility. We must see that the application of our doctrine is as important as the integrity of our doctrine. We must quit measuring our worth by the size of our budgets, credentials on our walls, or butts in the chairs, but by the way we equip and encourage our members to adventurously engage strangers outside of the moat of our churches. If we are to start making disciples like Jesus and planting churches like Paul, then we must not limit ourselves based on what we believe we are entitled to but surrender to the Holy Spirit as an unstoppable force.

In reading this book, you will notice that it gets personal. I have lived most of my life in the margins, and my tone may reflect it. Many illustrations are from my own life. People who know me will tell you that I have a way of saying hard things in ways that stick. It is never my goal to offend, but I also will not sanitize my language for the sake of being nice. You should also know that I did not write this book to turn the heads of academics or politicians. My intent is for its application to go from the elders' table to the Communion table to the kitchen table. I speak not just for myself but for the many marginalized who are often told to move on and not take things personally. But it is personal. And I ask you to take it personally.

This is when my *sueño* will be achieved: when our Great Commission zeal is matched to the Great Commandment—feeding the poor, loving the stranger, defending the oppressed, clothing the naked—and we begin to see the Great Community on earth as it is in heaven.

> Then your light shall break forth like the morning,
> Your healing shall spring forth speedily,
> And your righteousness shall go before you;
> The glory of the LORD shall be your rear guard.
> Then you shall call, and the LORD will answer;
> You shall cry, and He will say, "Here I am."
> ISAIAH 58:8-9

This is the justice revival. This is the mountain I will climb, and this is the only hill I will die on. I invite you to join me on this journey.

Vamos, compañeros!

see the new samaria

CHAPTER 1

Recalibrating Our Vision

ONE OF MY FAVORITE MOVIES is *A Christmas Carol* (1984), based on the novel by Charles Dickens. Ebenezer Scrooge, a name that today has become synonymous with stinginess, is a curmudgeonly businessman who experiences a remarkable transformation. At the beginning, we see Scrooge walking down the street when he is solicited for help for the poor. His response is callous.

> "Are there no prisons?" he asks.
> "Plenty of prisons . . ."
> "And the Union workhouses?" demanded Scrooge.
> "Are they still in operation?"
> "Both very busy, sir . . ."
> "Those who are badly off must go there."
> "Many can't go there; and many would rather die."
> "If they would rather die," said Scrooge, "they had better do it, and decrease the surplus population."[1]

Shortly thereafter he is confronted by his deceased business associate, Marley, who expresses concern for his soul. Marley, who is wandering about as a troubled spirit, tells Scrooge that he will be visited by three ghosts. The first ghost recounts Scrooge's past and how business became his god. When the second ghost visits, he reveals the joys of Christmas that Scrooge has missed all around him. Before his departure, the ghost opens his robe and reveals two gaunt, dirty, and hungry children.

Scrooge asks, "Spirit, are they yours?"
"They are Man's," said the Spirit, looking down
upon them. "And they cling to me, appealing from their
fathers. This boy is Ignorance. This girl is Want. Beware
them both, and all of their degree, but most of all beware
this boy, for on his brow I see that written which is
Doom, unless the writing be erased."[2]

Scrooge demands that they be covered up. He doesn't want to see them any longer. They are not his problem. The ghost obliges but says they are still there.

People throughout all time have chosen to not see uncomfortable truths when confronted with them. We choose to look away or cover them up, but that does not mean they are not there. We might not be as crass as Scrooge and dismiss people by calling them "surplus population," but we, too, hedge ourselves from issues that cause dissonance.

This story is reminiscent of the many times in Scripture when Jesus opened the eyes of the disciples to see things that they had become blind to. Humans are contextual beings. We see and interpret things around us based on the culture and context of the time in which we are living. When the disciples began following Jesus, they viewed their theology and worldview through a very particular historical, societal, and political lens. Very quickly we begin to see Jesus turn everything on its head. It turns out that the disciples had a lot to learn.

We as Christians face the same problem today. As Christian church leaders, we all embrace a mission for our lives and our ministry, and the ways in which we live out the mission are influenced by our culture. The question we must continually ask ourselves is, *What* or *who* might I be overlooking?

My guess is that some of you will define the church's mission more in terms of evangelization—sharing the Good News with people around you, making disciples, planting churches, sending missionaries to the ends of the earth—and for good reason, as this is the Great Commission that Jesus left for us. Others of you might define the church's mission more in terms of loving people—showing compassion toward the suffering, serving your community, bringing justice to the oppressed. This, too, is essential, as it is the Great Commandment that Jesus left for us.

As I stated in the introduction, both of these facets of the mission are essential. Unfortunately, we as Christians have done a poor job of executing both at the same time. The tendency of many churches is to lean more toward one, and in my experience in full-time ministry, as the population of our country has shifted, many churches have leaned into the evangelism mandate while the Great Commandment to love our neighbors has fallen to the wayside. We find ourselves wondering, just as the religious expert did in Luke 10, "Who is my neighbor?" and hope that the answer is people who are just like us. We've filled our churches with people who look like us, talk like us, eat the same foods as us—people who aren't going to make us too uncomfortable or make too many waves. The reality is that we're only willing to fulfill the Great Commandment halfway. I'll share more about this in chapter 7.

As you reflect on the way you are living the mission as a

Christian and as a church, think about the people who are sitting at your table and the values you emphasize. Who and/or what is missing? Many of us have blind spots that we don't even realize are there. It's hard to see what you don't know. Jesus saw the blindness in his disciples, and he was prepared to overturn centuries of conventional wisdom in order to recalibrate their vision.

Twelve Clueless Guys

In John 4, at the beginning of Jesus' public ministry, he gave his disciples a not-so-subtle command to look at what they did not want to see. Many people refer to this chapter as being about "the woman at the well," but I don't think it's as much about the woman at the well as it is about twelve clueless guys being taught an important lesson by their master. The story is about more than the woman's conversion and subsequent witnessing; while that aspect is very important, there is more to the story. Jesus used his encounter with the Samaritan woman as an opportunity to train his disciples, and we also have much to learn from this lesson in today's context.

In John 4:1-4, we see that Jesus intentionally chose to go through Samaria with his disciples. If you know the history and cultural context of the Samaritans and their relationship with the Jewish people, you'll understand why this decision was so significant. Jesus is teaching his disciples a lesson about the importance of mission over convention. While I'm certain that Jesus had the heart of the Samaritan woman in mind, he also had a bigger, broader lesson to teach regarding the disciples' predisposition to *not see* people that their worldview told them are not of value. Frankly, the lesson is as important today as it was then.

In 2 Kings 17, we learn that Israel and Judah were not keeping the commandments of the Lord, so God sent the people of Israel away from their own land into Assyria. So the area would not be depopulated, the king of Assyria brought people from Babylon, Cuthah, Ava, Hamath, and Sepharvaim, and they began to reside in the cities of Samaria instead of the children of Israel. We learn that the new residents did not follow the ways of the Lord, so God sent lions among them, which killed some of them.

As a result, the king sent one of the priests who had been carried away from Samaria back into the land in order to teach them how to live in a way that would please the Lord. Interestingly, while they did learn to fear the Lord, they still served their own gods "according to the rituals of the nations from among whom they were carried away" (2 Kings 17:33).

Here is an interesting point. When the Jews came back to the land, the Samaritans did not leave. Instead, they inhabited the section between Israel and Judah and were loathed by the Jews as unwelcome immigrants. But they had been living in the land for around two hundred years, so as far as the Samaritans were concerned, the Jews were the immigrants. My point is that both groups should have exercised a bit of pause relative to who were the landowners. The Jews forgot that they were at least remigrants to the area. Even though the Samaritans considered themselves worshipers of the Jewish god, the Jews never accepted them; in fact, the Jews hated them. The Jews called them dogs and declared that "righteous" Jews would not walk among them.

The Appointment That Should Have Never Happened

Taking this context into consideration, it's obvious that Jesus' encounter with the woman at the well is an appointment that should have never happened. Jesus, who was a prominent Jewish rabbi, should have never walked through Samaria with his disciples. Furthermore, when Jesus stopped by the well to speak to a Samaritan woman, he was going way out on a limb.

Jesus sent the disciples into the Samaritan city to get food while he stayed out by the well. He knew that the disciples would have resisted his decision to talk to this woman, just as they resisted when women brought their children to be blessed by him. He had to get rid of the disciples for this conversation to happen.

> A woman of Samaria came to draw water. Jesus said to her, "Give Me a drink." For His disciples had gone away into the city to buy food. Then the woman of Samaria said to Him, "How is it that You, being a Jew, ask a drink from me, a Samaritan woman?" For Jews have no dealings with Samaritans. Jesus answered and said to her, "If you knew the gift of God, and who it is who says to you, "Give Me a drink," you would have asked Him, and He would have given you living water.
> JOHN 4:7-10

The conversation between Jesus and the woman went on for a few more verses, but verse 10 is essentially the outline of their entire conversation. Allow me to break it down, since I'm amazed by the theology packed into this conversation.

1. First, Jesus clarifies the *what*: when he refers to "water," he's actually talking about the gift of God, the living water, which is eternal life.
2. Then he addresses the *who*: the source of the living water, the giver of eternal life, drawing attention to himself as the Messiah.
3. Finally, he refers to the *how*: in order to receive the gift of eternal life, you must ask the giver and he will give it to you.

In the dialogue between Jesus and the Samaritan woman, you can see the wheels in her brain turning as she tries to work out the theology and figure out who Jesus is and how he fits into the story of God that she's been taught. In fact, she asks him for the "living water" before she even understands that he is the Savior. After he points out her sin and she comes to realize her need for the salvation he brings, she doesn't need to ask again. The work is done.

At this point, the disciples return from getting food in the city. We can only imagine the looks of judgment that the disciples give this woman as she talks with Jesus. She walks away from the conversation under the gaze of the judgmental disciples, but it doesn't matter. She is a transformed woman.

The woman left that conversation no longer afraid of people's judgments. It is reasonable to speculate that she may not have been welcome at the water wells inside the city because of her reputation; therefore, what she did next was remarkable. John 4:28-39 says: "The woman then left her waterpot, went her way into the city, and said to the men, 'Come, see a Man who told me all things that I ever did.'" Her testimony was simple. The people immediately went to see Jesus, not because he revealed her sin—everybody knew her sin—but because they saw how the woman was transformed.

Mission over Convention

Now here is where the real lesson begins. The disciples wonder why their beloved rabbi was speaking to a Samaritan woman, as it goes against every social and cultural norm that has been ingrained in them. They are completely unaware that Jesus has just transformed a person's life. They return from the city with chips, cookies, and ham sandwiches (okay, maybe not ham sandwiches), while the woman returns with more souls to transform. I believe the visible contrast we see there was intended.

In this passage we see Jesus crossing cultures and breaking down barriers. Jesus could tell that the disciples were surprised, maybe even disappointed, that he was engaging in an interaction that shouldn't have happened. In response, Jesus tells them, "Don't you have a saying, 'It's still four months until harvest'? I tell you, open your eyes and look at the fields! They are ripe for harvest'" (John 4:35, NIV).

My father-in-law was a farmer for most of his life in North Dakota. It was literally his job to look at the harvest. All farmers know that they have to be vigilant, and in North Dakota it is even more important to be quick because the ground freezes for many months out of the year. No one living in farm country should need to be told, "Open up your eyes and look at the fields," which makes this figure of speech even more profound. The disciples were missing something important and didn't even realize it. Jesus was instructing them to open their eyes and see. He was not talking about the physiological working of the eye but the cultural filters that obstructed the sight of the image made in the likeness of God.

The Process of Unlearning

There are several reasons—theological, sociological, cultural—why the disciples couldn't see what Jesus saw. Everything about their history and their theology had predisposed them to see a certain way. One key consideration was geography. Samaria was in their Promised Land. "*We* are the chosen people, and *they* are on our land." Furthermore, God had instructed his people to be separate from the cultures around them that worshiped other gods.

In spite of all this history, Jesus still instructed them to open their eyes and see the Samaritans as people also made in the image of God. Jesus was asking them to challenge conventional thinking, remove their filters, recalibrate their vision, and re-sort through their cultural conventions and norms. His request is a shockingly tall order, overturning generations of rabbinic teaching and nationalistic pride.

The conventional wisdom of the day was leading to missional failure. The Abrahamic covenant called them to be a blessing to all nations. In both the Old and New Testaments, we read about instances when the Lord mandated that they love and accept the strangers in their land. The hate and resentment in their hearts could have resulted in them missing the opportunity to fulfill the Great Commission and the Great Commandment given to them.

Are we any better than the disciples? Do we have a point of view that causes us to overlook people? Come on, be honest!

Open Your Eyes and See

Before we can begin to engage the people around us, we must be willing to lift up our eyes and see. There have been significant demographic shifts in the last few decades (more on this in chapter 2), and how we view our neighbors will make or break our missional impact. We must see others as people made in the image of God—even a gift from God—to help us fulfill the mission of God to reach all people. Let me be clear: I am not saying that the New Samaria is a lost people who need to be saved. Of course, there are people of every nationality in our midst who don't yet know Jesus. But there are also some immigrants who come from parts of the world where Christianity is thriving, and they bring a spiritual vitality to immigrant churches in our community. Have you noticed? At the same time, however, majority-culture Christians need to be careful not to prioritize outreach to people who are culturally similar and forget about our neighbors who are different.

In order to rise up and see the New Samaria, we must do two things: (1) challenge our lenses with which we view the Kingdom and (2) recalibrate our vision to see people as God sees them. To recalibrate means to recheck, or to bring realignment to a tool according to a true standard of reality. As Christian leaders, we will all agree that Jesus is the true standard by which we measure everything and by which we live our lives. We all agree that God sees all people as made in his image—in theory. But when push comes to shove, our vision is stilted by cultural, political, economic, nationalistic, racial, and theological biases. It's not always evil, it's just the way we are wired until someone challenges our conventional norms.

Convention and Norms

Humans navigate the world around us based on subconscious social and cultural norms. I think of it like the unseen code behind the word processor. Most of the time these norms are good and help our society function smoothly. Social norms are what ensure that, for example, when a person enters an elevator with you, they'll stand on the opposite side. (If they were to stand directly next to you while the rest of the elevator is empty, things would get uncomfortable really fast.) Cultural norms dictate whether you hug and kiss a person when you first meet them, or give them a handshake. Sometimes it takes traveling to another place with a different culture to realize that some of our norms are not universal.

A few months after my move from Laredo to Austin for college, I was invited to a wedding by a white friend. In Latino culture, weddings are a big deal. There's lots of food, dancing, and friends and family sharing life together. I was so excited to be invited! On the day of the wedding, they took us downstairs after the church ceremony and gave us fancy little triangle sandwiches and sugar mints. I was impressed. I thought, *This is really high class that they're giving us this food before they lead us to the room for dinner and dancing.* Then my heart sank as I started to see people leaving the church. It was over! As it turns out, not all weddings are like Latino weddings. This is an example of discovering a cultural norm the hard way. For most of the people there, it was a happy event with nothing unusual about it. But it left me feeling lonely and confused. At my lowest point I even wondered if they were going somewhere to have the party without me!

Unfortunately, sometimes these social and cultural norms result in prejudices and biases against people who are different than us. For example, some people learned along the way that you shouldn't pass through certain neighborhoods because the people there are different and dangerous. Others come to accept certain smells and tastes as "normal," while those different from what you're used to come to be seen as "weird" or "smelly." We accepted those ideas as truth, and as we grew up, we continued to make unconscious decisions about who we associate with based on assumptions that we never thought to challenge. It begs the question: What happens when convention becomes malware? What happens when it becomes the enemy of mission?

The Two Harvests (Mind the Gap)

The harvest that the disciples had their eyes on was the only one they knew—their own people. This is the harvest Jesus alludes to when he says, "Do you not say, 'There are still four months and then comes the harvest'?" (John 4:35). It's similar for us today. Oftentimes the people we reach by default are those we already associate with. They are friends and neighbors and coworkers. We go to barbecues together, we know what kind of food they like, we laugh at the same jokes, and we are comfortable entering into spiritual conversations with them. It is absolutely good and right to reach these people. It is part of our mission.

But who is in this second harvest? The Greek text here is very emphatic that there is a contrast between the two harvests. Jesus is referring to this second harvest when he continues, "I tell you, open your eyes and look at the fields! They are ripe for harvest" (John 4:35, NIV). This field that is ripe for harvest is the Samaritans. The Jews didn't cultivate them. They didn't water them. They didn't even like them. But Jesus makes it clear that others tilled the Gentile mission field that he is now asking them to see, accept, and consider as God's children.

This passage in John 4 contains a prophetic message for us today. We live in what I call the "New Samaria," a place in which the second harvest is right in front of us. In the United States, I call us "Samericans," but the same idea applies no matter where you live. The Samaritans of today are the people living among us who have been marginalized, ignored, treated unjustly, or looked down upon. Oftentimes they are immigrants from other countries who are viewed as strangers and sometimes made to believe they are not welcomed here. We are not familiar with their customs, or we don't understand their language. Their second- and third-generation offspring were born here, but they are still viewed as "other" because of cultural differences or the color of their skin. Their foods smell funny to us, and we don't know how to dance to their music. Whether our uncomfortable thoughts toward them are conscious or subconscious, our lack of association with them speaks volumes about our respect (or lack thereof) for them. This might be hard to hear for some, but if we are being honest with ourselves, we need to admit that we all have biases against people who are different than us. It will be difficult to move forward if we can't admit that this is true for all of us.

One time at a large national conference I was eating lunch with a group of Hispanic leaders. After lunch we were walking out of the cafeteria when one of the majority-culture leaders called to one of our Hispanic leaders and asked if he could please clean off the table so they could continue their conversation without the table mess. The whole Hispanic team pitched in to clean off the table and left without saying anything. It's interesting that this leader couldn't conceive of a Hispanic person being there without table-cleaning responsibilities.

It was a very unfortunate mistake, but there really were fewer than twenty ethnic minority leaders compared to hundreds of majority-culture folk. The Hispanic leaders were gracious and took it in good humor, but this story points out the need to confront our biases head-on and unlearn the stereotypes that have been engrained in us. Case in point: Don't presume that because there is an ethnic minority/immigrant person around, they are the "help."

Ethnic and cultural diversity is a blessing that is here to stay, so we should move forward with a sense of urgency. In John 4, Jesus is not asking us to abandon the harvest we are familiar with, but he is saying that a bit of intentionality (as he demonstrated with the Samaritan woman) can pay huge dividends. He is saying that there is another mission in the margins that he cares for and is urging us to "mind the gap."

The Missional Matrix

Anyone involved in international church missions might be tempted to argue that we as a church *are* reaching people who are different than us by sending missionaries all over the globe to share the Good News. Of course, this work is good, and I'm not encouraging us to abandon this part of the mission. There is a place for it. But we also need to recognize that we don't have to go very far in order to find people who are different than us here.

A team I worked with created a graphic that I've adapted to help us understand where people fall on a matrix of near and far, similar and different. It's called the Missional Matrix. If our mission is to reach *all* people, we need to recognize where we have excelled and where we have fallen short.

MISSIONAL MATRIX

DIFFERENT

ENDS OF THE EARTH *GLOBAL MISSIONS* Challenge: Reaching different people who are far from us in a cross-national, cross-cultural setting OTHER COUNTRIES, CULTURALLY DIFFERENT	**SAMARIA** *THE NEW SAMARIA* Challenge: Reaching different people who are near to us, building relationships across cultures, and choosing accommodation over assimilation OUR NEIGHBORHOOD, SCHOOLS, WORK, CULTURALLY DIFFERENT
JUDEA *CHURCH PLANTING* Challenge: Reaching similar people who are far from us, building relationships and trust OTHER NEIGHBORHOODS, OTHER CITIES, CULTURALLY SIMILAR	**JERUSALEM** *LOCAL CHURCH* Challenge: Reaching similar people who are near to us, moving beyond the superficial to the spiritual OUR NEIGHBORHOOD, SCHOOLS, WORK, CULTURALLY SIMILAR

FAR ← → NEAR

SIMILAR

As you can see above, there are four areas of evangelistic focus, all of which fall along the matrix of either similar or different, near or far. The top left quadrant is where global missions would fall—focusing on those who are different and far. The bottom left quadrant is where church planting falls—focusing on people who are culturally similar but far from us. The bottom right quadrant is where our local church work falls—focusing on people who are culturally similar and near. All three of these are important and included in our mission as Christians. However, the area I have chosen to focus on in this book is in the top right quadrant—the area that focuses on people who are different and near, the place

I refer to as "the New Samaria." This is the area that I believe our church is failing to reach, the people that God is calling us to open our eyes and see.

American Missional Gap

In America we have focused so much on reaching the harvest that we can see—those people who are similar to us—that we have missed the second harvest. We have become excellent at reaching Americans near and like us by creating trainings and conferences aimed at reaching our lost comrades, as well prioritizing those who are far and different by consistently funding and sending people from the West to "exotic" locales with the gospel. Subsequently, we are missing the opportunity to reach the Samaritans in our midst—the immigrants, refugees, the poor, ethnic minorities, the people who have been deemed invisible or "surplus population."

To be clear: I am not against missions to people who are far away and different, but we who do remain must live as missionaries in our own country. The stakes of failing to reach the ends of the earth are high if our church ceases to be salty in its own backyard. It calls into question what we have to offer the world if we can't even reach the "other" in our own neighborhoods.

Interestingly, Jesus did not go into long conversations about the disciples' personal preference, prejudice, privilege, and misogyny, though they certainly played a prominent role in their dismissal of the woman at the well. Instead, Jesus demonstrated what a man on mission with the Father looks like—he engaged in transformational work. His attitude was juxtaposed to the disciples being off mission: They were self-sabotaging their ministry, overlooking a key future harvest, and trivializing the mission of God.

This should truly grip our hearts. Jesus commanded them to "see" because the souls of valuable human lives depend on it. In fact, the vitality of the church depended on them reaching all nations and peoples. Just as Jesus demonstrated what true mission looks like, so must we engage in this transformational work. But we must also be vocal about why this work is important. While some of us may get uncomfortable with conversations about prejudice, privilege, and preference (I will refer to these as P3), we as the family of God need to talk about them more. (More on this in chapter 3.)

Every summer, adults and youth board planes and fly to other countries for short-term mission trips. Their objective is to do their part in living out the Great Commission, sharing the gospel "to the ends of the earth"—and hopefully having a cross-cultural experience that impacts their worldview. Many of us have experienced trips like this; it has been part of the evangelical experience for decades. This movement toward short-term missions began in the 1960s and grew dramatically in the 1980s and 1990s. Nowadays, it is predicted that about two million Americans participate in short-term mission trips every year.[3] Unfortunately, however, after returning home, many people abandon the missionary mindset and return to their comfort zones.

I have been asked many times by people in the margins why it is that many Christians feel the need to fly across the globe to interact with people groups that can be found on the other side of our city! For example, according to the Joshua Project there are eighty-five people groups technically defined as "unreached" here in the United States.[4] With the movement of people groups being as prevalent as it is today, a similar phenomenon can be seen in other mission-sending countries as well.

My contention is that the way the church has historically viewed missionary work may not be as effective today. I feel particularly fervent about changing the church's approach toward missionary work because we open ourselves up to criticism when we export a strategy that may not even work in our own country. There needs to be a healthy synergy between home and foreign mission work. The example we give to other sending countries must have integrity. The mandate in Acts 1:8 is no longer a geographical line, from here to "there." The people from "there" are here, and we need to adjust our paradigm accordingly. We still need to reach the greater world; however, today, chunks of that greater world live in our neighborhoods. Whether through migration, immigration, education, or work opportunities, God has brought the world to us. I believe God is calling us to open our eyes and see. Once we recalibrate our vision, we will begin to see our neighborhoods as a new kind of mission field.

It's easy in today's cultural context to conflate immigrants, refugees, and ethnic minorities with law and politics, thus viewing this topic through a political filter. While politics and government do play an important part in ensuring justice for the oppressed, I don't believe that politics should be our primary filter. Here in the United States, for example, the question for many Christians becomes more about who should be in this country, who shouldn't be, national security, and which group wields more control, rather than seeing all people in God's image. It pains me when people believe the solution lies with one political party over another. No political system is perfect. Politics is the process by which a society actualizes its ideals, and as such it is almost by necessity always in flux. Therefore, politics makes for an unreliable filter through which to reliably discern current cultural reality. As Christians, our primary filter when looking at these issues should always be *mission*, not politics. It is our job to speak into it with compassion and justice at the forefront of our minds.

I urge us to keep the mission clear in our minds. Putting mission first means we may well be misunderstood, viewed as disloyal, or even attacked by those who make loyalty to a political party primary. Be prepared. Our allegiance must be to our King and his mission. If we truly want to see transformed people and communities in our midst, we must keep the GC3, which I mentioned in the book's introduction, top of mind: the Great Commandment and the Great Commission help build the Great Community.

I believe many of you reading this book have seen the need for holding the Great Commission and the Great Commandment in balance in order to see great transformation. Too often lay Christians are afraid to challenge the system. We think that bigger and greater people have this all figured out. If this is you, be courageous enough to speak up when you see the vulnerable being ignored or taken advantage of! In the book *The Leadership Challenge*, Kouzes and Posner say this about the importance of challenging: "Challenge is the crucible for greatness. Every single personal-best leadership case involved a change from the status quo. Not one person achieved a personal best by keeping things the same. Regardless of the specifics, they all involved overcoming adversity and embracing opportunities to grow, innovate, and improve."[5]

• • •

My actual reason for loving the story of Ebenezer Scrooge is because of his transformation from an aging, lonely man to a generous, joyous soul who, with the time he had left, more than made up for his years of selfishness by giving of himself for the benefit of humanity. In order to begin to love others, he first had to open his eyes and see them.

Before we can begin to love our diverse communities, we must first see the community the way God sees it. If we are not even willing to look, how can we love? It starts by obeying the order to see the New Samaritan mission field and recalibrating ministry paradigms to make room for this new harvest. Let us see ourselves, see the New Samaria, see the will of God, and join him on the road to transformation.

REFLECTION

Consecrating Prayer: Lord, help me open my eyes to see what you want me to see. Even if I can't do anything about it now, please let me see what you see.

Head Work: If you were to have the angels of Christmas past, present, and future visit you in one night, what would they reveal about your life among the poor and the vulnerable?

Heart Work: Has there been a time when the Spirit convicted you to see or do something for a stranger, and you quickly quashed the prompting of God?

Hands Work: When God puts someone in your path who is from a different culture or socioeconomic level than you, strike up a casual conversation and just spend five minutes listening to them. Learn something about their family and their lives in the community. Later when you are spending time in prayer, remember them by name.

RESOURCES

- Book Suggestions: *The Next Evangelicalism* by Soong-Chan Rah; *Strangers Next Door* by J. D. Payne; *The God Who Sees* by Karen Gonzalez; *The Dangerous Act of Loving Your Neighbor* by Mark Labberton

CHAPTER 2

The Demographic Tipping Point

There is a new U.S. demography on the horizon. The demographics in several key areas are shifting in the early 21st century. They aren't your father's population trends, and the church must be positioned to better serve the changing culture.

**SAM S. RAINER III,
"SEISMIC CHANGE IS COMING TO THE
CHURCH IN A NEW DEMOGRAPHY"**

IN HIS BOOK *CANOEING THE MOUNTAINS,* Tod Bolsinger uses the story of Lewis and Clark and their journey into uncharted territory as a metaphor for the current moment we face as leaders in the church. When Lewis and Clark finally arrived at what they thought was a waterway to the Pacific Ocean, they found the Rocky Mountains stretching out as far as their eyes could see. All of their assumptions about the terrain ahead were wrong. Not only was the land different, but they had to adapt to the people on the other side. They had to decide at that moment whether they would give up and go back or adapt and continue. Lucky for them, they had Sacagawea, who had been born Shoshone and was now the wife of Toussaint Charbonneau, who had been hired as their guide through the mountains. Sacagawea proved to be an incredibly valuable asset (even more so than her husband), as she was able to serve as their interpreter and translator. As Bolsinger says, "Sacagawea was not venturing into unexplored territory, she was going home."[1]

The landscape of the United States has changed dramatically over the last fifty years. In addition to the reality of a post-Christian culture, what some refer to as a farewell to Christendom, we are also facing a shift in demographics that has caused our cities and communities to look and feel very different. Some Christians have, intentionally or unintentionally, been able to isolate themselves from this change, but that can only go so far. We cannot deny it, and we cannot hide from it. In this chapter we're going to dive primarily into the changing landscape of the United States. But our world is experiencing dramatic migration and population shifts. The UN reports that as of 2018, "the world is witnessing the highest levels of displacement on record."[2] The issues I raise here are likely relevant in your setting, no matter where you live.

I believe we are at a moment in which Christian leaders need to take a good look at the terrain ahead and ask ourselves if we are ready to adapt. And just as Lewis and Clark learned, adapting will mean giving up some of our power and centering voices of color, who will be more adept at navigating the terrain.

My, How Things Have Changed

In the 1990s, Rick Warren's well-known Saddleback Church was one of the first churches to adopt the purpose-driven and seeker-friendly church paradigms that quickly became popular in the United States. The church created an evangelistic target named "Saddleback Sam," a middle-aged white man who is well educated and financially well off, has a wife and two kids, and is self-satisfied and skeptical of organized religion. At the time of the church's founding, Orange County was monocultural (mostly white) and upwardly mobile, so this fictitious personality—Saddleback

Sam—was exactly who they needed to cater to in order to maximize their growth potential and develop discipleship models that were relevant. This is the epitome of the "homogeneous unit principle" (more on this in chapter 10), a concept more popularly known as "birds of a feather flock together." They were a majority-culture church in a monocultural community that adopted a strategy to reach people who were just like them.

Even though that was many years ago, many majority-culture churches have similar targets today. Maybe they are catering to their surrounding community, or maybe they are just doing what feels comfortable. My question is, What happens when someone walks into your church who looks nothing like Saddleback Sam? Many of us in the non-majority culture have been in that situation, when we walk into a church that feels like it was not meant for us. When the church's programs and models cater to the majority culture, people who don't fit that mold feel unwelcome, misunderstood, and out of place.

Not surprisingly, the demographics around Saddleback Church began to drastically change decades after its founding. Now, Orange County has transitioned from a monocultural community to an ethnically diverse community. And guess what? There is no longer any reference to Saddleback Sam in their mission statement; instead, the focus is on evangelism, discipleship, compassion, and justice issues. The church has adapted and done the work of welcoming Samerica into its midst.

It's time for a new kind of target! Perhaps it's an immigrant who is culturally religious, comes from a working-class family, and lives in fear of getting stopped by the police because of their immigration status. Or maybe it's a young ethnic minority who has faced discrimination throughout their life, struggles to receive quality education, and doesn't feel entirely welcome in the US even though they were born here. Or maybe it's someone who has faced poverty and homelessness and can't seem to get ahead in life no matter what they do. Either way, none of these people would feel at home at a church filled with Saddleback Sams.

Let's be honest. Change, especially change relative to root memories of our old stomping grounds, is difficult to accept. In our mind's eye the home we grew up in and the school we went to still look the same. When I went to seminary, I worked at Interstate Battery of America. They were a blessing to work for, and even forty years later I still dream about the place. A while ago I went to visit the office and few remembered me. Life may go on, but we enshrine memories that we do not want to be interrupted by reality. The fact of the matter is that the city or the country we grew up in probably looks and feels very different now than it did decades ago, and oftentimes our resistance to the change is a direct result of nostalgia and sentimentality. But Jesus has told us to open our eyes and see the harvest! It is not too late to dream with our eyes open about how the church could be revived by embracing the changes. Let's not allow the powerful force that is nostalgia to get in the way of our call to mission.

Demographic Shift and the Issue of Immigration

Only the most self-deceived Americana romanticist denies the impact of minority population growth and the impact of immigration on our country and the church.[3] Even if the trend of immigration were to be frozen (which I do not believe it will), we are on a trajectory to reach a demographic tipping point in this country, and there is no turning back. We must open our eyes and see the magnitude of the mission we are facing as a church.

For many Americans, much of what we know about immigrants is heard on TV or radio or read on the internet. Most of us likely already know this, but just a friendly reminder that not everything we read or hear about immigrants is accurate. It is not uncommon for statistics about immigrants to be misrepresented in the media or for anecdotal stories to be passed around as a way of inciting fear about the "strangers" among us. We must attempt to ensure that what we hear or read is accurate before allowing it to influence our opinions or feed into existing stereotypes. I would also highly suggest reading up on the history of immigration trends and global migration patterns before forming opinions about contemporary immigrants.[4]

Let me give you an example of how nostalgia and misinformation have a significant effect on attitudes about immigration. It is a known fact that the United States is a country of immigrants. Ninety-nine percent of our population has an immigrant history— that is, everyone except the few whose ancestry is entirely Native American.[5] Interestingly, however, Americans today seem to have different feelings about the immigration of our nation's early years than they do about the immigration of today. Americans tend to romanticize the early eras of immigration, when brave souls arrived at Ellis Island in search of the "American Dream," as opposed to current immigration, which some view as an influx of potentially dangerous strangers who want to take advantage of the system. Those opposed to contemporary immigration are quick to point out that early immigrants (i.e., their ancestors) came the "legal way," whereas many immigrants today are coming illegally. This, however, is a common misconception. Immigration in the early days was a much simpler process, so almost everyone who arrived was admitted, usually after just a few hours of processing. It is an unfair comparison, given that many immigrants today often don't even have a line in which to wait.[6]

For centuries America has relied and thrived on immigration. The biggest difference between early immigration patterns and more recent trends is that immigration from the nineteenth and early twentieth centuries was European dominated, while in the last fifty years we've seen an increase in immigration from Latin America, Africa, and Asia. This change was brought on by the 1965 Immigration and Nationality Act, which did away with a long-standing national origins quota system that favored immigrants from Europe and replaced it with one that emphasized family reunification and skilled immigrants. Since that landmark immigration law was enacted in 1965, over fifty-nine million immigrants have come to America. Immigrants and their US-born children make up 26 percent of the population, and this number is expected to rise to 36 percent by 2065. In 1965, 84 percent of Americans were non-Hispanic whites. By 2015, that share had declined to 62 percent and continues decreasing every year. The reality is that, as a result of immigration and childbirth patterns over the last fifty years, the nation's racial and ethnic composition has changed dramatically.[7]

Most noteworthy is that, according to the most recent census information, the total white population in the US has declined for three consecutive years in a row. This loss is enough to counter any gains that happened in the last decade, meaning that the 2010–2020 decade would be the first one in our nation's history in which the white population did not grow.[8] Furthermore, the median age for the Hispanic population is about a decade younger than the white non-Hispanic population, and since the white population is older and not replacing itself at a higher rate, the younger age of the Hispanic population will only accelerate the demographic change in the coming decade.

The most important takeaway here is that the US is diversifying even faster than predicted, and the country's population growth rate is being propelled by racial and ethnic minorities. The country's overall population will feel the impact of these shifts. Non-Hispanic whites are projected to become less than half of the US population by 2055 and 46 percent by 2065. No racial or ethnic group will constitute a majority of the US population. Meanwhile, Hispanics will see their population share rise to 24 percent by 2065 from 18 percent today, while Asians will see their share rise to 14 perecnt by 2065 from 6 percent today.[9] Many other groups claim the demographic tipping point will happen as soon as 2045.[10]

Everything happening in the United States, including immigration patterns, is not happening in a vacuum. It's actually connected to a global phenomenon of population growth and push and pull factors in migration. Understanding global context is vitally important if we want to be informed citizens of the world and of God's Kingdom,[11] as global migration is going to have a huge impact on the future of the United States. Demographic changes have been working their way through the American social system slowly but surely for fifty years now. But since it is like a slow train moving down the tracks, people almost forget and disbelieve its inevitability. If we look carefully, we can clearly see it is here. In 2017, the total enrollment in public elementary and secondary schools was majority minority.[12] Politically this shift has been flipping cities and states from one political party to another, according to the Brookings Institute.[13]

The business world has a metric that requires them to adjust to these changing demographics to stay in business. Businesses must absolutely prepare themselves to capitalize on the shift because their metric for existence—i.e., money—is merciless. On the other hand, the church generally has been a late responder to change. The church's soft metrics—such as numbers of conversions, baptisms, church plants, gospel initiatives—allow for a measure of denial or the ability to redefine a missional win to suit our needs; that is, until missional failure becomes undeniable. More often than not churches don't see the need to adapt until it is too late.

As we head into a future with no ethnic majority—a future

where diversity and multiethnicity is the norm—it is imperative for Christians to be intentional about adapting if we want to pass the church forward to future generations. Christians love to talk about all people being created in the image of God, and yet history has shown that sometimes we are slow to affirm the dignity inherent in those who are most vulnerable. The church has more than once lost its light, failing to respond to social problems that affect people made in his image. The Christian church in the US split over the issue of slavery, with some churches justifying it by all sorts of devious theological twists. Some of our most respected seminaries at one time excluded people of color and justified it under the flimsiest of theological premises. When Japanese Americans were interned in camps, many people in the church were silent about the civil rights injustices happening in front of their eyes. Many Christians and church leaders did not support the work of Martin Luther King Jr. because the movement he represented disrupted privilege and made many Christians uncomfortable. A more recent example of injustice is the family separation occurring at the US-Mexico border, an issue on which many in the church have been silent. The sad thing is that, according to a survey done by LifeWay, less than 2 percent of evangelicals have ever heard their pastor preach about the biblical response on the treatment of immigrants.[14] By not preaching on the Bible's treatment of immigrants during a time when the issue of immigration is a national headline, we are missing the opportunity to teach about the biblical perspective and leaving people to draw their own conclusions based on what they hear from media and politicians. This is a major failure of Christian leadership, and real people have suffered as a result.

It's easy, in retrospect, to see where the church went wrong in its response to many social issues in the past, whether through silence, inaction, or active marginalization of ethnic minorities.

Hindsight is always twenty-twenty, but seeing clearly—and engaging in a biblical response—in the present is still challenging for some. Unless you're Rip Van Winkle and just waking up after twenty years of being asleep, there's a good chance you've seen the demographic changes happening around you. Seeing is the first step, but the way we respond to them is key. Some people have the privilege of ignoring the shifts and creating a bubble around their families to provide perceived "safety" from differing views and cultures. The other option is to embrace the change, realize the value of diversity, and work to ensure that everyone made in the image of God is being treated with dignity, regardless of what we think about the application of immigration law.

One time I was speaking at a Christian conference about the issue of immigration and the church. Afterwards I was approached by an older white woman who asked why I was making it easy for "those people" to come here. She said that America was founded by good white people, and I was just helping them destroy all the good that this country had become. "These people only get welfare and have babies, so of course they are outnumbering white people." She said George Washington would be turning over in his grave if he knew what America was becoming. She concluded by saying "we" paid for the church to be what it is now, only to be giving it away to people who never paid their dues. "Our island of safety is shrinking," she said, "and I am afraid for our children."

This was not the first time, and definitely not the last time, that someone expressed their disapproval of my work and their fear toward the changing demographics of this country. Many of us who do this kind of work in Christian circles face criticism on a regular basis from people who allow stereotypes, fear, and ignorance to define their opinions of those who are different. Some might consider the above example to be an extreme view, but I strongly believe that this woman was speaking the fears that many majority-culture Christians in the US have, only many do not say it out loud. She likely was not too satisfied when I said our only hope was to let down the drawbridge and welcome them into the house of God, as fellow people made in the image of God.

Research has shown that in the US, older white Christians are more likely to hold a perspective that we must protect ourselves against a foreign minority out of fear that our culture or values are being threatened.[15] People with this viewpoint often harbor anti-immigrant sentiments because they believe immigrants will spoil our cultural or religious values. I do believe that every sovereign nation has a right to define and defend its borders, but it's hard for me to accept that Christians would hold this callous view due to the biblical mandate to love our neighbors, welcome strangers, and spread the gospel, even if it's in our backyard. But somewhere along the way, some Christians began to equate nationalist values with Kingdom values, believing that there is something special about their country that needs to be protected. It is this nationalistic thinking that has hindered the church over the centuries: first in Jerusalem and then in Asia Minor, Rome, and the rest of Europe. Lamenting the presence of outsiders as if it is the death of our church and/or country goes directly against God's commandment. It can be a delicate matter balancing our earthly and heavenly citizenship, but in the end, "we ought to obey God rather than men" (Acts 5:29). In the book *Autopsy of a Deceased Church*, Thom Rainer uncovers twelve consistent themes among churches that have died. The book's overall conclusion is that churches die when the focus of the church turns from being outwardly focused to being inwardly focused. To be inwardly focused means developing disciples inside your church; to be outwardly focused means serving the community outside your church, even as the community around you starts to change. Rainer's contention is that in order for a church to live, it must be serious about *both* the Great Commission *and* serving their community. Those that don't do both eventually develop "Great Commission amnesia."[16]

It doesn't happen all at once. It happens little by little as a church begins turning inward, ignoring the people around them, turning away from the very people who could have been the life-blood of the church, propelling them into the future. Our beautiful edifices become our mausoleum brick by brick until they are empty. They become like the magnificent cathedrals of Europe, serving more as tourist attractions rather than places of spiritual vitality.

Friends, today we have gotten so caught up in doing what we've always done, doing what is familiar, that we have forgotten to look and see where the Father is at work around us. Jesus saw what his Father was doing and joined him. We must do the same, even if it is outside of our comfort zone.

Of course, there are some Christians who have been working for many years to shed light on justice issues surrounding our changing demographics. In *Christians at the Border*, Daniel Carroll makes one of the best efforts at presenting the Bible's teaching on immigration and urging Christians to respond in a Christ-centered way. He cites organizations in the United States that have collaborated on a national level to engage churches and leaders with immigration issues. For example, the National Association of Evangelicals (NAE), World Relief, and the Evangelical Free Church of America's (EFCA) Immigrant Hope (immigranthope.org) have collaborated together to develop conferences and training for Christians.[17] The NAE and World Relief focus primarily on immigration advocacy. Immigrant Hope plays a more grassroots role, as they train denominations and churches to practically serve immigrants by providing basic legal advice. Another important organization is the Immigration Alliance (theimmigrationalliance.org), whose primary focus is helping churches build capacity to serve immigrants rather than pressing toward a political solution. There is need for both approaches: advocacy *and* also building capacity to serve churches that seek to be the hands, feet, and witnesses of the Lord. I'll go into more detail about this in chapter 4.

Making the Paradigm Shift

This book is about more than just immigration, but it is a focus of this chapter because statistics don't lie. More people than ever in history live in a country other than the one in which they were born.[18] In the US, the demographic tipping point is near, and the church will need to adapt. What will it take for majority-culture Christians to make the paradigm shift in their thinking? What kind of changes will it require to our seminaries and denominations to begin investing heavily (in prayer and resources) to reach and empower the marginalized already within our borders?

For some of you, this is nothing new. You have seen it coming, and you are ready to get to work. For others, it is still hard to wrap your mind around, and you would rather stick with what you know. Throughout the remainder of this book, I hope to show you why leaning into the demographic tipping point and working to reach the New Samaria will not only bring you life but will also bring the church back to life. The Lord has promised that the church will not fail. Join us in the margins. That is where the future lies.

REFLECTION

Consecrating Prayer: Lord, help me to see what you are doing in my neighborhood, city, and country, and may I not let fear or apathy get in the way of viewing everyone with dignity. Help me see it as your invitation to love, reach, and learn from different kinds of people who are made in your image.

Head Work: Do an objective search of your own neighborhood's demographics. Check out the school district's diversity on their website. Check the districts in neighboring neighborhoods. Compare that to the diversity of your church. Who is not present at the table in your church community?

Heart Work: How do you feel when you hear statistics about the changing demographics of your country? What are your honest thoughts about immigrants and the diversity of cultures and languages around you? Have you allowed God's heart toward "strangers" to penetrate your own heart?

Hands Work: Take a drive through a neighborhood near you that is different—perhaps ethnically or socioeconomically—and get a feel for its resources or lack thereof. On one Sunday go to a church in that part of town. Take some time to process what you see, hear, and feel.

RESOURCES

- Visit City-Data.com to learn about the demographics and economic statistics of your city.
- Visit justicemap.org to visualize race and income data for your neighborhood, county, state, or the entire US.
- Book Suggestions: *Christians at the Border* by Daniel Carroll; *Welcoming the Stranger* by Matthew Soerens and Jenny Yang; *A God of Incredible Surprises* by Virgilio Elizondo

CHAPTER 3

Justice Revival

GOD'S MISSION HAS NEVER WAVERED. While God is steadfast in his love and mercy, we as humans have been prone to wander. I love the hymn "Come Thou Fount of Every Blessing," as it sings to the beauty and steadfastness of God in his dealings with us. In one stanza, it speaks directly to the heart of any honest child of God.

> *Oh, to grace how great a debtor*
> *Daily I'm constrained to be!*
> *Let Thy goodness, like a fetter,*
> *Bind my wandering heart to Thee.*
> *Prone to wander, Lord, I feel it,*
> *Prone to leave the God I love,*
> *Here's my heart, oh take and seal it,*
> *Seal it for Thy courts above.*

This was my nightly cry as a young believer. I had found the greatest treasure and vowed to never be untrue; but already inside I could feel the pull of fleshly gravity. The hippies were after me. There were times when I would do his good work in my own strength and after a while the results of my efforts became undeniably putrid. I had to return to focusing on God's mission, not my own. The hymn captures the transparent fear most, if not all, of us have as followers of Jesus.

God's mission has remained the same—from the mandate to Adam, Eve, and Noah to "be fruitful and multiply," to the mandate to the disciples to go and "make disciples" and "love your neighbor as yourself." We are to be people who live our lives with an external focus on increasing God's tribe, loving our neighbors, and passing on our faith. As in the hymn above, our hearts have also wandered. We have too often made the mission about ourselves and wasted efforts focusing on the wrong things. Christians have spent so much time and effort disagreeing about issues like cultural engagement, political involvement, evangelism strategies, and biblical orthodoxy. While these conversations are important and necessary, we cannot engage productively if our spiritual vitality has been lost. I believe what we need is to enter into a time of spiritual renewal, during which we can repair what has gone wrong, heal our divisions, and refocus on God's primary mission. Mission is inextricably connected to spiritual renewal. As Paul Pierson writes in his book *The Dynamics of Christian Mission*, "The Holy Spirit comforts, empowers, and equips believers. His empowering and equipping are primarily to carry out the will of God throughout history, both in the Church and in the world. Therefore . . . any experience of renewal that does not lead to mission is incomplete at best."[1]

When spiritual renewal is divorced from mission, it results in Christians who may go to church on Sunday, put money in the collection basket, and attend an occasional Bible study, but fail to look beyond themselves and their families. It results in Christians who believe in the Great Commission and the Great Commandment but have handed off that work to pastors, ministry leaders, and missionaries. Here is what many people forget: the Great Commission and Great Commandment are not abstract mandates; they are mandates for every man, woman, and child. Our ministers were never meant to be our designated holy people. God will hold each person accountable for their part in the execution of his mission. I believe we have reduced church to what is manageable. We have settled for a God who we don't think can work the way he did in the Bible. What we need is a rapid, rushing wind of transformation and genuine revival. Fulfilling God's Great Commandment and Great Commission together means working not only among those who are like us but also among those in the margins, among the vulnerable. This can feel uncomfortable and unpredictable for some—but this does not give us license to avoid it. In this chapter, I will lead us through what I believe we need, and what we need to repent of, in order to align ourselves with God's mission.

What We Need: A Justice Revival

The purpose of chapters 1 and 2 were to help us open our eyes to "the other harvest," which I also call "the New Samaria"—a group that is moving from the margins to the center at a rapid rate. In order to align ourselves with God's mission amid the demographic tipping point we are experiencing, opening our eyes and seeing is the first step. But what must we do next?

The next step is revival, but not just any revival—a justice revival. When I lead workshops across the country and mention that we need a revival, everyone nods their head and declares, "Amen!" But then, when I specify the type of revival we need—a justice revival—heads stop nodding and eyebrows start to raise. This is not what many Christians think about when they think "revival." But indeed, I argue, a justice revival is the inevitable result of seeing what we have been blind to for so long.

In today's political and social context, *justice* is a loaded word. I wish this weren't the case, as justice is at the center of God's heart. It literally is the quality of being fair, equitable, and balanced, which everyone should agree is a positive principle that we should strive for as human beings. Unfortunately, in Christian circles it has become a word that has strong emotional implications and elicits both positive and negative reactions beyond its literal meaning. It is often associated with a certain political party and specific social movements, to the point that I believe many Christians have forgotten its true meaning. It goes hand in hand with compassion, mercy, and love. Justice is a biblical mandate that many Christians overlook.

When I say we need a "revival," I don't mean the planned readjustment that some of our churches do every year in which we draw a circle around ourselves and recommit to being good and holy. The revival we need is *not just* of an individual becoming more spiritually holy, praying more, engaging in spiritual disciplines. I say this with much trepidation, but we have been there and done that. The prayer, evangelism, and humbling part of revival are always in order, but there are areas in need of repentance that have only been superficially dealt with. I believe that we are in a different season and are facing a national need for repentance that we've been ignoring for a long time, and now it is impeding our very ability to be on mission with God.

God forcefully describes this kind of justice revival in Isaiah 58:

Is this the kind of fast I have chosen,
    only a day for people to humble themselves?
Is it only for bowing one's head like a reed
    and for lying in sackcloth and ashes?

Is that what you call a fast,
a day acceptable to the Lord?
Is not this the kind of fasting I have chosen:
to loose the chains of injustice
and untie the cords of the yoke,
to set the oppressed free
and break every yoke?
Is it not to share your food with the hungry
and to provide the poor wanderer with shelter—
when you see the naked, to clothe them,
and not to turn away from your own flesh and blood?
Then your light will break forth like the dawn,
and your healing will quickly appear;
then your righteousness will go before you,
and the glory of the Lord will be your rear guard.

ISAIAH 58:5-8, NIV

Repenting from Our Sins

What we need is the revival in Isaiah 58, calling people to repentance from callousness and injustice toward marginalized people. The sins resulting from preference, privilege, and prejudice (P3) have hung around our neck as a nation for a long time. We are in a spiritual battle that requires us to enter into uncommon repentance. We need to move beyond personal holiness to a commitment to see the image of God in other people. We need to turn collectively from our sins resulting from preference, privilege, and prejudice (P3). This goes beyond political, social, and theological redress—even though that is important. Isaiah 58 offers a corrective to a typical revival in its intentional call to seek sacrificial compassion and justice for the oppressed.

This revival is a reboot to our missional call. It helps us live out a biblical Jubilee[2] that resets our spiritual and relational debt to

God and each other. It frees us to live as one unified church before God. It is a "revitalization movement"[3] that helps us fully engage our rapidly changing culture and yield fully to the power of the Holy Spirit. This is not a biblical adaptation but a recommitment to the way we live out our sanctification in this world as God always intended. It is a commitment to live as a royal priesthood of all people together: race, gender, nationalities, and generations.

Over the last twenty years I have spoken at many different denominational conferences and consulted with churches about the need to recalibrate our vision as a Christian church. Sadly, I've encountered a great number of statements that put our mission-drifted malaise on full display. While it can take many forms, I see it displayed the most in relation to sins that result from preference, privilege, and prejudice (P3). Let me give a few examples.

PREFERENCE

Once I was serving at a church in the Midwest that had a large population of migrant field workers living around them. I suggested that they organize a service for the migrant field workers as a way of making them feel welcome in the community. We would offer food from their home countries and invite them to stay for fellowship. One of the women who would typically help plan such an event objected to the idea because it made her uncomfortable. "Their food has a strange odor," she said, "and what if they drop red Kool-Aid on the carpet?" This woman cared more about her preferences and the cleanliness of the carpet than about God's mission.

Preference is pretty innocuous. Most people prefer certain types of activities, food, and smells over others, and having those preferences is not inherently sinful. The phrase "birds of a feather flock together" describes the phenomenon that people with the same sort of tastes and interests tend to hang out together. We've all experienced it, whether through cliques in school or friend networks as adults. But it's when we refuse to acknowledge the existence of our comfort zone, and when our preferences begin to set the rules for how we relate to our neighbor, inside or outside of church, that it becomes downright sin.

PRIVILEGE

There is a progression from preference to privilege. Privilege starts hitting at the advantages that are granted to certain groups of people within a system or culture. There are many areas of privilege, and many people live with at least one. If you have the right attributes or fit into the favorable social groups, then you generally have an advantage that is out of your control and that you didn't ask for. For example, a white person might experience favorable treatment in housing or banking simply because she is white; a man might get more opportunities to advance in certain industries, or get paid more, because of his gender; a store owner might view a customer with suspicion merely because she looks to be working class rather than business class. Having this privilege, which you didn't ask for, isn't evil. It is possible to use our privilege for God's purpose. But when we expect things to happen for us just because of who we are, or expect less for others because of who they are, that is when privilege becomes dysfunctional and evil begins to creep in.

One time I was organizing an informal theological training session for ethnic minority pastors so they would be able to write and defend their official ministry credential. A white, male, ordained pastor I was working with said to me, "Will this not diminish the efforts of the other men who went to seminary and got ordained formally?" While he did not intend for his question to be offensive, the idea behind his question reveals the level of privilege he is swimming in without even realizing it. The ethnic minority leaders participating in my training would never have been able to attend a formal seminary here in the United States because of educational and language barriers, yet they were gifted and called and had natural leadership abilities. By offering them theological training, they would be better equipped to lead their churches and bring the gospel of Christ to others in our community. But instead of getting on board with how this approach would advance the Kingdom of God, the ordained pastor was questioning whether it would diminish the efforts of the pastors who went to seminary—without even recognizing the structures in place that keep underrepresented minorities out of our seminaries. Did he believe, deep down, that one group is more important than the other? These thoughts and ideas are typically subconscious and aren't always said out loud, but they exist in more people and places than we'd like to admit.

PREJUDICE

While privilege is sometimes in the domain of the subconscious, prejudice is the intentional belief that one group of people is more important than another. This can take many forms within the Christian church. Most often it shows up as subtle or indirect statements, questions, or actions that cause minorities to feel unwelcome in the church body. Sometimes it shows up as outright xenophobia (fear of people from other countries) and discrimination.

I have more stories than I'd like to admit about Christians, both lay members and leaders, who were against ethnic minorities and immigrants joining their churches. In one particular case, I was helping a large church recruit an ethnic minority leader. We had an excellent candidate, but the senior pastor rejected him because of the color of his skin. His church was predominantly white, and the senior pastor did not think the elders would approve of him.

Optimists like to believe this kind of outright discriminatory behavior doesn't occur anymore in churches, especially among church leadership. Unfortunately, what many don't understand is that preference and privilege are so prevalent in the psyche of our culture and churches that eventually outright prejudice is bound to rear its ugly head.

Structural P3

When there are flash points in the news about abuse, racism, or blatant unmasked hate, many of us recognize that as obvious injustice. Certainly, there have been some political, social, and even theological efforts to address and redress obvious injustice. But much more work needs to be done to root out unfair and unjust structures that exist in our world. In *Beyond Racial Gridlock*, George Yancey refers to this as the structuralist viewpoint, which rests on the idea that we are affected by the social structures in which we live. So even when people do not intend to be racist, the society we live in will still perpetuate racism.[4] For example, studies have shown that black students tend to receive lower scores on standardized tests and are underrepresented in advanced courses in school. This has nothing to do with their innate academic ability. Rather, black and Latino students are more likely to live in low-income neighborhoods with a lack of resources, are less likely to have teachers or counselors they trust or who look like them at school, and are more likely to be left out of gifted and talented programs.[5] These disparities cannot be blamed simply on individual racism; instead the problem is embedded into our society—the way schools are funded, the way teachers are trained, and the way standardized tests are created.

This is just one example of a deep-seated structural bias that disproportionately affects people of color, ethnic minorities, immigrants, and marginalized people. Injustice is all around. We may not have individually created it, but in many ways, we unwittingly participate in it. If we do not acknowledge the injustice, then we are perpetuating it. And if we are perpetuating it, then how can we do anything about it? And if we don't do anything about it, as Christians, what does that say about our theology? Do we truly believe everyone is created in the image of God?

Jesus holds up the story of the Good Samaritan as an example of how we are required to act as believers. The Good Samaritan did not cause the traveler's injury, yet he still saw it, acknowledged it, and did something about it. Conversely, some of us have walked on the other side of the road so as not to be personally confronted by things that we don't want to acknowledge. I believe this is why many Christians have not been able to fully understand and embrace the mission of reaching the marginalized, the future of the American church. We have approached it without repentance. Some have approached the New Samaria as an interesting phenomenon. At best, we wonder how to get "them" to be more like us. At worst, we don't think about them or try. They are not our problem.

I believe the American evangelical church in general (though certainly not all evangelicals) is on autopilot. When we start thinking that the mission of the church is to develop better programs for our people instead of about reaching the vulnerable and the lost, we begin the slow descent to spiritual death—death by comfort. Missional drift. We saw it happen in Scripture and in the early church, and it is still happening today.

Missional Drift in Scripture

Missional drift is certainly not unheard of in the history of Christianity. Scripture has many examples of when God's people drifted from the Lord's mission. The book of Isaiah chronicles a very dark time in the history of God's people. The kingdom

of David had split into two kingdoms because of Solomon's dis-
obedience. Judah, the southern kingdom, had barely withstood an
attack and was clearly shaken. The northern kingdom, Israel, had
been defeated and marched off into captivity. While in captivity,
the teaching of Jewish elders started to become more sacred than
the Torah. Traditions that had been passed down, even if they con-
tradicted the words of God, held more sway. In Isaiah 29:13 (NIV),
the Lord said:

> These people come near to me with their mouth
>   and honor me with their lips,
>   but their hearts are far from me.
> Their worship of me
>   is based on merely human rules they have been taught.

Jesus refers to this passage in Matthew 15:3-7 (NIV), when the
Pharisees questioned Jesus about why the disciples were breaking
the traditions of the elders. Jesus replied, "And why do you break
the command of God for the sake of your tradition? . . . You hypocrites! Isaiah was right when he prophesied about you."

The disciples' lack of ability to see the Samaritans as a mission
field, while connected to their lack of spiritual vitality, was more
so a result of the preference, prejudice, and privilege that had been
passed on to them by their culture and religious traditions. As
I mentioned in chapter 1, hatred for the Samaritans went back
many generations. They didn't individually create the system, but
they benefited from it. If they could not even see the Messiah,
whom they claimed to be waiting for, how could they see the
opportunity to be his ambassadors to a group that tradition had
pitted against them? The Messiah and the mission were right in
front of their eyes, but they could not see them because of their
spiritual blindness.

Our Blindness Equals Israel and the Early Church

Some of the mission-drifted malaise that we read about in the Old Testament is certainly alive today, though it manifests differently in today's culture and society. If you're not paying attention, it's easy to miss. Christians have figured out wildly successful methods for creating good programming, planting new churches, leading Bible studies, and doing evangelism—all while missing the mission field.

Indifference toward the marginalized in the midst of "counting our blessings" for ourselves will destroy a house as easily as an attacking army. It was this attitude that was condemned by the prophets. Many have heard the story of Sodom and Gomorrah and believe their destruction was the result of the practice of homosexuality. In reality, it started with the belief that the blessing of God was their heritage alone, which led to indifference toward the suffering and oppression of marginalized groups (sins of omission), as well as inhospitality toward visitors, idolatry, and power abuses (sins of commission): "Now this was the sin of your sister Sodom: She and her daughters were arrogant, overfed and unconcerned; they did not help the poor and needy" (Ezekiel 16:49, NIV).

Over the years we have witnessed the evangelical movement become more inwardly focused. I see us circling the wagons out of fear that we are being attacked. Outsiders like immigrants, ethnic minorities, liberals, globalists, and people who will spill red Kool-Aid on our carpet are to be kept at bay. Americans like to speak about our national and religious prominence as our spiritual heritage, and Christians evoke it in their prayers, politics, and psyches. We turn to politics for solutions and hope that if we elect more politicians to advance our moral agenda, we will see revival. We try to press down the sinfulness of the world by convincing others they need to "be good," when we can't even live up to that standard.

Ya, Basta! ("Enough Is Enough!")

I call for the vote! We don't need politics, another conference, workshops, or even this book! What we need is to see how broken, naked, and prone to wander we are, as the hymn indicates. I'm not saying that good things are not happening anywhere. God's Spirit is at work in local contexts in pockets of our country, and I will give many examples of this in later chapters. However, as a nation and as the evangelical movement, we are *not* seeing the changing mission field because we are looking inward and backward, not forward.

I believe it is time to pay the spiritual bill if we want to be used by God. Without this wholesale spiritual purgative exercise, I doubt we will see what we need to do. It's time to call for a justice repentance revival. You ask, "What will we get out of it?" Life!

I believe we stand in the same place as Judea when Isaiah made this prophecy in Isaiah 58:1-12. God called Judea to move beyond personal holiness to a commitment to show compassion and justice to the vulnerable people among them. Follow along with me as we distill this important passage and consider its message to us.

God: (verses 1-2) Somebody, please tell my people they are lost. They strive hard for perfect doctrine and pray for justice but care little to live it out.

Takeaway: God will call out nations for not matching their walk with their talk.

God's people: (verse 3) God, why won't you get with the program? Did you not see we fasted? We also had our annual revival with all the trimmings, and you missed it!

Takeaway: People will be offended and complain because they think their programmed efforts are sufficient.

God: (verses 4-5) I wasn't present because it wasn't real. You still use your status to take advantage of the vulnerable and exploit your workers. All you really did was check off the box, pat each other on the back, attend long meetings, and give money to help the food bank or your old clothes to the clothes closet. But you didn't even invite the poor, the hungry, and the oppressed to your festival.

Takeaway: God views our surface-level, programmed efforts as fake repentance and as self-promoting.

God: (verses 6-7) This is what I'm talking about when I talk about repentance and revival. Help those who are unjustly detained. Feed the hungry. Confront people who look down on those from the "less than" neighborhood. Invite the outsiders to your house and make them feel welcome.

Takeaway: God is actually calling for an uncommon repentance involving justice for the marginalized. We need to welcome anybody made in the image of God into the house of God and invite them to sit next to us.

God: (verses 8-9) If you do these things, then you will explode with real life. You will shine forth with righteousness and not worry about what is behind you because I will have your back. Then you will call for me, and I will answer.

Takeaway: You have been looking for righteousness in the wrong places. The work of doing justice and mercy will bring you life. God will see you, hear you, and answer you when you are seeking justice for the oppressed.

God: (verses 10-12) If you give liberty, if you help feed the hungry, if you help those who are hurting, then you will be a light in the darkness. It is not easy work, but God will guide you, satisfy you, and strengthen you. You will be a rebuilder of ruins. You will raise up old foundations. You will be a repairer of broken walls and a restorer of paths.

Takeaway: Don't take God's blessing for granted. The if-then structure to this passage shows the conditional nature of a revival. Do not think short-lived, surface-level justice and mercy efforts are enough. Your work must be continual, and relying on God is essential to make it through.

I had always thought that personal holiness, prayer, spiritual disciplines, and evangelizing were the disciplines that pleased God. And to be fair, they are indeed important. Yet, Isaiah 58 blew me away the first time I studied it. Why did the Lord give us this added *corrective of compassion and justice for the marginalized* in Isaiah 58? Here is why it is necessary.

1. *It presses repentance beyond the comfortable.* The Lord's complaint in Isaiah 58:3 is that their repentance is just a show and only based on some religious program. It was not from a humble and broken heart. It cost them no inconvenience, much less was it aimed at helping the vulnerable. The very people who would have benefited from a real revival, the poor and the broken, probably were not even invited. The repentance party was only for the holy huddle.

2. *It puts the focus on people over programs.* Programs can be extremely helpful, but when people serve the program, rather than the program serving the people, it all becomes an exercise in self-justification. People start comparing themselves to other people. On the other hand, the best

revivals I have seen and heard of are messy. People don't necessarily act right. Process charts and minute-by-minute time sheets lay on the floor, underneath the people who are bowing down before God. They don't care who is watching or how they may be offending the stage managers.

3. *It insists that love of neighbor is essential.* The corrective of justice and compassion in Isaiah 58 is an intentional admonition to people in that they can't say they love God and see loving their neighbor as optional. This added corrective is an important component that must be genuinely owned in our effort to reach the New Samaria. This corrective is not new, but at times it may have seemed unnecessary, especially when dealing with our own folk, people who look like us. For the Great Commission to have relevance and connection to the New Samaria, we must break our systems and integrate these time-honored and biblically mandated love additives. If we were missionaries in another country, perhaps we would be more open to learning and loving. But because we are in our own country, we expect assimilation to our way of seeing things.

The Orthodance

When good doctrine (orthodoxy) is matched by vigorous living out of that doctrine (orthopraxy), we see transformation. I call this the orthodance. In every frontier of the gospel, the Great Commandment lived out in compassion and justice for the oppressed sets up the Great Commission. People want to know you truly care about them before you share your wonderful plan for their lives. Our walk must match our talk!

I wrote in chapter 1 about the GC3, which means that when the Great Commission (Matthew 28:19-20) is matched by the

Great Commandment (Matthew 22:36-40), we never fail to see the Great Community be transformed (as in the book of Acts). By transformed community, I don't just mean a transformed local church. I also see a community around the church that has been transformed by the efforts of the church. The church serves, loves, and meets people's needs. All of this can only be kept in balance by reliance on the Holy Spirit rather than some program disconnected from the reality of life around the church. We need to ground all our work on good doctrine, but theologians must give equal respect to practitioners who "live out" their faith by all means, including compassion and justice. The orthodance is truly a dance we must all learn.

Rodney Stark, in his book *The Rise of Christianity*, meticulously documents this dance. Christians in the first centuries during the plagues made it a central part of their mission to care for the sick. Africa, which has lately become the center of mass conversion, is rooted in compassion and seeking justice for the oppressed. Stark writes: "I believe that it was the religion's particular doctrines that permitted Christianity to be among the most sweeping and successful revitalization movements in history. And it was the way these doctrines took on actual flesh, the way they directed organizational actions and individual behavior, that led to the rise of Christianity."[6]

While we put much emphasis on guarding pure doctrine, Stark's key point is a critique of the worship of doctrine for doctrine's sake. Doctrine needs to "take on flesh" in order to be healthy. This is the essence of James's exhortation in 2:14-24, where he claims that faith without deeds is dead. Some call it the "walking out" of doctrine or cultural engagement. Without living out that doctrine, our faith fails to lean into the necessary witness of deeds to the watching community.

This is the fresh wind we need today. My prayer is that God

will free us from the parts of the dead weight of ossified religion that want to condemn, imprison, and keep "good" people safe. Free us to love and serve people before we ask if they are legal. Free us from our attachment to political parties. Free us to allow sinners to act like sinners among us without being offended at their indiscretion. Free us to bring them to church and allow them to keep their children with them as long as they like before we hurry them to their proper Sunday school class. Free us to miss a church event to take a family to some needed government service. Free us to increase the church budget so that we can meet people's unexpected needs in the same way we budget for catastrophic building repairs. Free us to love outsiders, even if they spill a little red Kool-Aid on the carpet.

Preacher, Now You're Meddling with Me

If you have gotten to this point in the book without throwing it away (thank you!), you may be wondering if you are called to do the work of ushering in a justice revival and where you should start. Lay Christians—and even church leaders at the local level—tend to think there's someone else who should be starting this, like the denominational leaders or the head pastors. To that I say, nonsense! You are the church. Yes, I'm talking to you! Don't wait for permission to start justice work among people in the margins. You are closer to the battle lines than anyone. Just lift up your eyes and see. God will lead through you.

This book is targeted not to the academics but to Christian families as they sit around the kitchen table. In the next few chapters, you'll read about regular churches, regular people like yourself, who said yes to God and began justice work in their churches. And what will you get out of it? I will tell you: a rejuvenated, recalibrated, relevant, disciplemaking philosophy for the future. We are never more alive than when we are on mission with God.

May God make you like the vessel filled with oil that never goes empty! Stay connected to the Lord, and it will be so.

REFLECTION

Consecrating Prayer: Lord, help me see my religious efforts through your eyes. Help me, Lord, to see that there is so much more to the spiritual life than what I have made peace with if I join your mission to seek the good of the vulnerable.

Head Work: How does Isaiah 58:1-12 challenge the typical view of a revival? Check your assumptions about the extent of your church's involvement in serving the lost, the poor, the stranger. What are some ways you or your church could stretch your comfort zone and begin exercising compassion or seeking justice for others?

Heart Work: Have you settled for a spirituality that is focused on yourself, without looking for the joy and power offered in Isaiah 58?

Hands Work: Identify a family in need that you can go serve, whether through your church or a different church. Maybe there is someone you've encountered at work or school. Ask what practical needs you can meet, such as providing a meal, clothing, or school supplies. Get to know the family's story.

RESOURCES

- Subscribe to the Chasing Justice podcast (chasingjustice.com), led by a team of people of color who mobilize a lifestyle of following Jesus and rebuilding a just world. You can also read their blog at chasingjustice.com/blog.

- Book Suggestions: *Generous Justice* by Tim Keller; *God Loves Justice* by Jessica Nicholas; *I'm Still Here* by Austin Channing Brown; *The Myth of Equality* by Ken Wytsma
- Bible Study Suggestion: *Conversations in Justice: Small Group Study Guide for Generous Justice* by M. Travis Simone and Tim Latham

love the new samaria

CHAPTER 4

Extending Our Vision of God's Kingdom

Do not forget to show hospitality to strangers, for by so doing some people have shown hospitality to angels without knowing it.

HEBREWS 13:2, NIV

IN SANTA BARBARA, CALIFORNIA, in 2005, Shoreline Community Church was experiencing a radical change in their community and in their church. The city's demographics were changing rapidly as more immigrants moved in and white people moved out to the suburbs. Their predominantly white congregation was aging, and there were no longer any children running in their hallways. So little was happening at the church that some neighbors, they later discovered, thought the building was abandoned.

Then one day, a few members opened their eyes to see. They decided to pioneer an outreach to neighborhood children, many of whom were from immigrant families. A Wednesday Bible club and Sunday morning kids' program meant playful voices were being heard again. They began to reach out to the children's families, who began to attend services, and the church's original congregants began to grow in love for their community. They got to know their names and their stories: Martha and Jose, both working long hours, anxious about their latchkey children; Geraldo, who was caring for his aging mother; Victoria, struggling to keep her family together after her husband was deported back to Guatemala.

When the church became outwardly focused, they saw spiritual vitality. Getting to know their neighbors allowed their hearts to soften and grow in love toward people they once ignored. This act brought renewal and life back to their church.

The Adventure Begins with Love

This story of Shoreline Community Church is a beautiful example of how opening our eyes to the New Samaria leads us to love, which is where the real adventure begins. In part 3, I will be telling stories of churches that chose love and as a result saw an extension of God's vision in their communities. But first, we need not look further than Jesus for an example of joining the Father where he's at work, despite controversy, popular opinion, or long-standing traditions of the elders.

After the conversion of the Samaritans in John 4, Jesus and the disciples remained for two more days. I'd like to think they were having a grand fiesta. It must have started off awkwardly because of their different dietary staples and cultural traditions, but nevertheless, they stayed. Jesus wanted to teach them an important lesson, and it's no wonder that it took a few days; Jesus was addressing deep-seated biases that were impeding their missional vision, resulting in blindness to the purposes of God for the world.

After two full days of a fiesta in the Samaritan village, Jesus and the disciples traveled to Jerusalem. They arrived on the Sabbath, and Jesus healed a man sitting by the pool of Bethesda who was hoping to be healed from thirty-eight years of infirmity.

Instead of a celebration, Jesus was questioned by the religious leaders for healing on the Sabbath. I wonder if the disciples saw the contrasting reaction. The Samaritans worshiped Jesus, but his own people questioned him for healing a man who had been in affliction for nearly four decades. Here is how Jesus defended his actions:

1. My Father is always at work (even on the Sabbath). JOHN 5:17
2. I look to see where the Father is at work and work only there. JOHN 5:19
3. Because the Father loves the Son, he shows him where he is at work. JOHN 5:20

This is why Jesus was so effective. He rested in the realization that his Father already had it all figured out and was already working. So Jesus didn't have to figure out a five- or ten-year plan. Jesus did the hard work of looking to see where his Father was already at work, and that's where he focused his time, even if others did not agree.

What a novel idea! This is a real challenge for many, especially Americans who love to come up with plans for everything (not to mention avoid things that are controversial). The problem is, usually our plans are too small. Not only has Jesus clearly called us to open our eyes and see the harvest, but he's also called us to look to where the Father is at work. When was the last time you asked yourself, *Where is God at work around me?*

What if this demographic shift is from God? What if this is the Father at work, and what if we should see the movement of people around the world as his doing? If this is the case, then reacting in fear, resisting, and trying to limit their growth is actively working against God.

Let's Not Repeat History

In the United States, we have a brutal history when it comes to the treatment of nonwhite people, and many Americans are not very good at remembering our history. Most are aware of the genocide committed against Native Americans during the period of colonization, or the evils enacted against Africans during the periods of slavery, but there's way more than that, and much of it has happened in the not-too-distant past. Just in the last one hundred years, due to the pseudoscience of eugenics, abortion was used to help limit African American population growth.[1] Native American children were removed from their homes,[2] and many Native American women were involuntarily sterilized.[3] There were also many different efforts to woo lighter-colored people from Europe to migrate to the US, while restricting people of color from coming.[4] Our country has a strong history of trying to erase or reduce the number of ethnic minorities living here in order to keep people of color in the minority.

Nevertheless, the demographic tipping point is still on its way. White Americans are not replacing themselves, and the minority fold is growing quicker than ever before. The fact is, without immigrants our country would have huge problems finding workers, funding the Social Security system, and maintaining our economy. Not to mention, our churches would have fewer ambassadors for the Lord!

What if this growth is part of God's plans to reach the world? I believe God is exercising his prerogative to determine a nation's boundaries and the time of their position or privilege in the world. That is something God preappoints for himself. Consider Acts 17:26-27: "And He has made from one blood every nation of men to dwell on all the face of the earth, and has determined their preappointed times and the boundaries of their dwellings, so that they should seek the Lord, in the hope that they might grope for

Him and find Him, though He is not far from each one of us." In the summer of 2018, I stood on the very hill in Athens where these words were spoken by Paul. Paul was not staying long because he was on his way to the city of power, Corinth. Athens was no longer the political power, but it was considered a center of learning and the pursuit of truth. The irony is that while they liked new ideas, they didn't like outsiders. Sound familiar?

Paul seized the opportunity to share the gospel with the Athenians. He started by connecting their culture and religion. He cited an altar they had set up with the inscription "to the unknown god" and proceeded to introduce them to the known God. Paul continued, telling them that God sets the times and boundaries of their dwelling, declaring that God uses the changing of borders and the rearranging of people groups for an evangelistic purpose, so that they may "grope for Him and find Him."

That groping might very well be the way many immigrants and refugees describe their journey to this day. I truly believe it is by God's design that people from all over the world are living among us. This is the Father at work. Are we ready, as Jesus said, to work where the Father is at work?

We Fear What We Don't Know

A Hispanic friend of mine told me about an incident that happened to him when he was serving as an assistant pastor. He is an immigrant from Mexico, but at that time he had been living in the United States for several years as a naturalized citizen. One day he was walking the halls of his church when an angry church member (who was white) burst out of the senior pastor's office. The church member looked at my friend, who just so happened to be walking by, and yelled, "Like him! Why is he here? Why doesn't he just stay in his own country?" The church member and head pastor had been engaged in a discussion about the increase of immigrants in their community, and poor Ricardo, who was at the wrong place at the wrong time, was the unfortunate target of the church member's anger.

What the angry church member did not know was that the Hispanic pastor was leading a thriving ministry that was on its way to doubling the size of the church. His work was not front and center, so at the beginning, it wasn't obvious to the white congregants who were not paying attention. This is how God's work in the margins works. Majority-culture folks sometimes have to remove their blinders and be intentional about seeing. At my friend's church, eventually the Hispanic ministry grew so much that the ethnic composition of the church switched! It is vitally important for us to extend our vision of what God's Kingdom looks like. If we remain indifferent toward or fear those who are different, then not only are we personally harmed because of our sin, but we are also missing out on experiencing God's transforming power.

Contact Hypothesis and the Power of Proximity

I chose to study social work for my undergraduate degree at the University of Texas in Austin, partly because I knew that I loved people and wanted to find a career compatible with making disciples. So I took classes in counseling, community development, and social psychology, which I loved because of their practicality.

It was during that time that I first came upon the "contact hypothesis" of Gordon Allport. The book he published in 1954, *The Nature of Prejudice*, described the idea that the most effective way to reduce prejudice, stereotyping, and discrimination between majority and minority group members is by interpersonal contact. During that time policymakers and social scientists were especially interested in the implications of interracial contact, given the desegregation of the military, schools, and other public institutions. It was in everyone's interest to figure out how to reduce the negative impact of these human behaviors.[5]

I really didn't need Allport to tell me that being in close contact with people helped to reduce prejudice; I was living it! When I left Laredo for the first time and moved to Austin to live "among the hippies" and lots of other people who were different than me, my fears of the unknown subsided, and I began to understand that they were people just like me.

In the decades after Allport's book was published, social scientists have continued to study how the contact hypothesis impacts prejudice, even beyond race. It has proven to be successful in improving relations between all kinds of groups in conflict; however, there is one important determining factor. The successful reduction of prejudice is more likely to occur when there is some kind of shared characteristics or goals between the groups, such as a perceived common interest.

Several Christian authors have expounded upon this theory in the context of our Christian faith. In the book *Divided by Faith*, Michael Emerson and Christian Smith refer to the importance of having a network of sustained interracial relationships, rather than just occasional contact, to achieve unity in the church.[6] Rev. Dr. Brenda Salter McNeil also discusses this idea in her book *Roadmap to Reconciliation*, and John Perkins has also written much about this in his writings about race and justice.

Jesse and the Man at Walmart

A few years ago, I wrote a parody (of sorts) of John 4 (Jesus' encounter with the woman at the well) called "Jesse and the Man at Walmart," in which I attempt to help readers reimagine the story in today's context. If Jesus were alive today and touring your city with his disciples, who might he choose to approach in order to illustrate how his Kingdom extends beyond what we like to envision? The person I chose to represent the woman at the well is an undocumented day laborer standing outside a Walmart waiting for work.

Jesse was touring the city with his disciples Billy, Jerry, and Joel. One day he sent them into Walmart to get some food for their evangelistic swing. While they were gone, he met an undocumented man standing at the day-laborer corner eating some tacos and waiting for work. Jesse went to him and said, "*Hola, amigo,* can I have one of your tacos?"

The hombre looked down, then in broken English said, "Why are you talking to me, and why do you want some of my tacos? The only time your kind of people talk to us is when you want us to work for you. We stand on this corner and people laugh and spit at us. They call us 'illegal' and 'wetbacks,' so why do you now call me 'amigo'? And now you want my tacos, señor?"

Jesse said, "If you knew who asked you for your taco, you would have asked me and I would have given you food that would give you eternal life."

The hombre said, "Señor, are you feeling okay? You don't have any food in your hand to give life. How can you give me food that will help me live forever? You need to get out of the sun, señor. We don't need your invisible food."

Jesse said, "If you would ask me, I would give life to you."

The hombre no longer looked down but directly at Jesse. "Life? We don't need the kind of life your people offer. We have holy rollers and hallelujah people come to this corner and talk to us all the time about eternal life.

They tell us we need to go to their churches to get right with God. They tell us we should not be here, but then they take us to their home to cut the grass, take out their trash, and paint the walls. In their house they treat us like we are invisible, but we see what they are watching on TV and the kinds of magazines they are reading. Sometimes they get drunk and send us away without paying us. Is that the kind of life you are talking about?"

Jesse said, "Show me your green card."

The hombre said, "I don't have a green card."

Jesse responded, "You have said well you don't have a green card. You have come to this country illegally five times."

"Señor, are you a curandero? We are so confused about religion and where we should go to church. Los Americanos tell us to go to their churches but then they treat us like we are basura. Some of their radio evangelists call us thieves and criminals, and then they want us to convert and go to their church. We are crying out to God because we live in fear. We are only here to help feed our families and live a quiet life."

Jesse said, "I came that you might have life and have it abundantly. If you come to me, I will save you and guide you. I know your pain. I was an immigrant in a foreign land as a child. I was rejected by my own religious people. I have overcome. I can feed you. I can give you true security. I can make your load light. I can give you real eternal life."

At that the undocumented hombre dropped his taco, saw Jesse as the Savior, and ran to tell his compañeros that he had found the Son of Mary and Joseph of the Bible on the corner at Walmart.

Billy, Jerry, and Joel came out of Walmart and saw Jesse talking to the man. They said, "Why are you talking to this man? They shouldn't even be here. You might be breaking the law just by talking to them. This is bad for our public relations."

Jesse said, "I have public relationships you have no knowledge about." (Joel wondered, *Did he find a PR agent we don't know about?*)

About that time a large group of people were coming around the side of the Walmart when Jesse said to the disciples, "Lift up your eyes and see the people who are made in my image. This is what the Great Commission is all about. Sometimes a little compassion opens doors for the Good News in ways no seminary training or PR will ever get you. If you want to reach people for the gospel, you are going to have to talk to the lawbreakers. You were once lawbreaking sinners. Quit looking down on them! Turn off the TV and radio talk show hosts and get a life. I came to seek and save the sick and not the healthy."

The people all sat around Jesse, and he gave them the food the disciples had bought and taught them about security, peace, and eternal life. They put their trust in Jesse and invited him to their barrio. They shared with him their chorizo, menudo, tortillas, and homemade salsa (not the fake stuff they sell at Walmart). Then Jesse healed all the people that were brought to him.

My purpose for including this parody is not to talk about the politics surrounding undocumented immigrants.[7] (Also, remember that not all undocumented immigrants are from Latin America. I simply use them in my story because this is closest to my context as a Latino from South Texas.) My desire is to illustrate two points.

The first is that Jesus loves, saves, equips, and sends everyone, even the most marginalized in our societies. In the United States, as well as other countries around the world, undocumented immigrants represent a group of marginalized people who are looked down upon uniquely because of their immigration status. I tend to notice a visceral response from majority-culture Christians when the topic of undocumented immigrants comes up, as if they are an exception to the "love your neighbor" mandate because of the fact that they broke the law. When I share this parody at Christian conferences, some members of the crowd get visibly uncomfortable. This is exactly why I like to share it. Jesus illustrated to his disciples in John 4 that he sees beyond what our cultural conventions teach us. Jesus' mission was to love and give life to everyone, especially those deemed by society as unworthy. Replacing the Samaritan woman with an undocumented immigrant in today's context causes us to confront our deepest biases and think about what sins we need to repent of in order to get on mission with God.

The second point I want to illustrate is the impact of proximity. One of the main learning points of John 4 is how Jesus initiated a conversation that should have never happened, since Jews and Samaritans did not associate with one another. But after the woman's conversion, Scripture tells us that many Samaritans believed in him. In fact, they urged him to stay with them, and he stayed for two days. Jesus was setting an example for his disciples in how fulfilling his mission requires breaking down ethnic and cultural barriers. Proximity is the most effective way to do that. Looking people in the eye and sharing the pain and issues of life changes how we see one another. The parody urges us to apply John 4 to today's context and think about undocumented immigrants as people made in the image of God—but the lesson can be applied to any person society views as "other." It is not "us" versus "them." We are all one body, imperfect as we are. Brothers and sisters, may we all have the courage to initiate relationships with people we've been taught to avoid. God will work in transformative ways.

God Is Always at Work in the Margins

Many years ago, I was having dinner with a dear friend of mine from New England named Ves Sheely when he shared a thought that sent me spinning. I believe I missed the rest of what he said during the meal. The words he shared were "Look for God's work in the margins. God is always at work in the margins."

I had an epiphany at that moment. I grew up on the margins of Texas and Mexico. I looked back and saw how the Lord sovereignly equipped me and even gave me a heart that could traverse the margins without being crushed like roadkill. In my work among the people in the margins—ethnic minorities, immigrants, and the poor—I have seen a great receptivity to spiritual matters, along with a simple and sincere faith. I have seen ethnic minority leaders and immigrants plant churches with little training, little ministry resources, and little affirmation from the entitled and endowed. For example, a study conducted by LifeWay Research demonstrated that Hispanic churches see similar patterns of growth and evangelistic effectiveness despite having fewer financial resources and training, as compared to church plants of all ethnicities.[8] Working in the margins for most of my life has given me a front-row seat to watch the modern-day equivalent of what the early disciples did with few resources and a lot of faith.

I want to make it clear that God is at work everywhere—both in majority- and minority-culture settings—and when I say "work where God is at work," I don't mean that you have to choose one over the other. The fields are ripe for harvest everywhere! What I am saying, though, is that for many Christians, it is easier to let the marginalized harvest fall to the wayside if we are not regularly engaging with one another (out of sight, out of mind). It is also common for majority-culture folks to assume that the poor and marginalized need help and swoop in to "save" them (savior mentality), failing to see the work that God is already doing there. The Lord is giving us all the opportunity to engage with the ends of the earth in our neighborhoods, which was not a possibility at other points in history. But be careful to remember: seeing and loving the marginalized is more than an exercise in compassion, as if we're checking off a "good deed" box. We must repent and seek biblical justice, as I discussed in chapter 3—not in some programmed way, but in an authentic way that brings transformation.

Let us also remember that the majority culture must not expect assimilation; rather, we must empower and learn from marginalized leaders, otherwise we will see a choking of ministry. I have seen the merging of the margins vicariously breathe new life into a ministry that was stagnating. I've seen old and weak hands strengthened when the marginalized are welcomed and empowered.

I've been blessed in my ministry career to witness and learn from many ethnic minority leaders who are working in the margins and having a big impact. David Gibbons is a Korean American pastor who planted a multiethnic community in Irvine, California, with no denominational support, paid staff, or other supporting entities. He just did what God told him to do. His vision was: "The future is already here; it is just on the margins." When he felt like an outsider, like he didn't fit anywhere, he decided to start a church for people like him—the misfits and the marginalized. Today, Newsong Church is a community that serves its neighbors and brings people into relationship with Christ, and it has expanded by launching locations in Mexico City, Bangkok, London, and India.[9]

Wilfredo De Jesús (known as Pastor Choco) is the senior pastor of New Life Covenant Church, one of the fastest-growing churches in Chicago. New Life is a multiethnic community with multiple locations aiming to reach the marginalized community, including the homeless, those suffering with addiction and prostitution, and young people in gangs.[10]

Some of my biggest heroes are African American Christian leaders who have had a long history of serving in the margins and have been the mainstay in honing the conversation of justice and compassion. Rev. Dr. Brenda Salter McNeil is one of my favorite speakers and authors who has spent her career equipping the next generation of Christian leaders to be practitioners of biblical reconciliation. She is associate pastor of Quest Church in Seattle, which is a welcoming, multicultural community that emphasizes both personal discipleship and justice for the oppressed. I have been heavily influenced by the works of Martin Luther King Jr., Rev. John Perkins, and my professor at Dallas Theological Seminary, Dr. Tony Evans. We have so much to learn from those who have been at work in the margins their whole lives.

• • •

I opened this chapter with the story of Shoreline Community Church in Santa Barbara, which chose to extend the vision of God's Kingdom through their community. The Shoreline Community Church of today is vastly different than what it was in the early 2000s. They have a vibrant Spanish-speaking congregation, and the English-speaking congregation has come back to life too. English- and Spanish-speaking kids chatter together in the halls. Tentatively at first, the two congregations have grown together. They regularly share meals and plan joint worship services, and they are working toward functioning as one multiethnic congregation. I'll share more about how Shoreline has exhibited their love for the New Samaria in chapter 6 and chapter 11, which are about embracing the pain of the marginalized and transforming their community, respectively.

What happens when a congregation decides to reach the New Samaria? God will expand their borders beyond what they could have ever imagined.

REFLECTION

Consecrating Prayer: Lord, help me love people who are different than me. Help me be bold and see things through their eyes. Help me develop a friendship with someone who is nothing like me.

Head Work: Think about the kinds of people you have befriended at school, work, or church. How many of them were of a different ethnicity than you? What kinds of things draw you into a friendship, and what kinds of things keep you away?

Heart Work: Due to the ideas passed on to them over generations, the disciples avoided associating with Samaritans. Think about the ideas passed along in your family and whether any of them have (consciously or subconsciously) caused you to avoid certain kinds of people.

Hands Work: Begin to frequent a restaurant of a different ethnicity than yours. Work to get to know the staff. Learn about their lives. Over time, trust and friendship will grow.

RESOURCES

- Find out your Proximity Index by visiting https://bit.ly /samariaproximity. This short survey will help you discover how proximate you are to the poor and provide suggestions, based on your positioning, on how to move toward greater activism.

- Book Suggestions: *The Power of Proximity* by Michelle Ferrigno Warren; *Beyond Colorblind* by Sarah Shin; *Roadmap to Reconciliation* by Brenda Salter McNeil

CHAPTER 5

Appreciating the Beauty of Other Cultures

*Consequently, you are no longer foreigners
and strangers, but fellow citizens with God's people
and also members of his household.*

EPHESIANS 2:19, NIV

AURORA, COLORADO, a burgeoning suburb just east of Denver, has seen a dramatic demographic shift from 85 percent white to 60 percent nonwhite within the past twenty-five years. In the mid eighties, New Life Church had relocated to Aurora from Denver when the city started changing and experiencing white flight. Then, in the early 2000s, once again the neighborhood around the church started changing, with Latin Americans, Asians, African Americans, Ethiopians, and Russians moving in. In the public schools, 128 languages were being spoken. New Life's pastor, Jeff Noble, knew that the church had once moved when facing similar circumstances, but he knew that was not the right approach. He, the elders, and others began to ask, "What is God wanting us to do?"

They began to talk, pray, and ask God to show them what they needed to change about their posture in order to begin reaching their rapidly changing community. They began attending conferences, reading books on multiethnic ministry, and studying the Scriptures. After a period of praying and seeking God, they felt led to officially adopt a multiethnic vision for their church and intentionally become a more welcoming community to other cultures. Slowly they began to see more diversity within the church, and eventually they opened their doors to a Hispanic church and a Korean church looking for meeting space. As those relationships grew close, they began to see opportunities to expand even more.

Roughly twelve years later, New Life now hosts four second-language services: Arabic, Filipino, Spanish, and Ethiopian/Oromo. These groups minister together, preach in each other's pulpits, worship together, and do outreach together. They also have people from thirty-five different nations attending their Sunday morning English services. Pastor Jeff Noble said in a recent interview: "Multiethnic church is so meaningful to me now. I can't imagine going back to a monocultural church."[1]

The process has not been simple or easy. As the church's diversity grew, some existing New Life members left, either because they were uncomfortable with the changes or they were leaving the community to more affluent areas. About an equal number were thrilled about the change! The big middle, maybe 50 percent of the congregation, were a little bit hesitant—mostly because they were unsure what this would look like—but through the teaching of Scripture and their trust in their leaders, they responded: "Okay, let's give this a try." Perhaps the most satisfying for Pastor Jeff has been watching hesitant members go on to become the church's biggest believers in its multiethnic vision.

What impact has this shift had on the church? They have discovered just how much they can learn from people of other cultures and have grown in their love for one another.

This, my friends, is the contact hypothesis in action. There is so much power in proximity. When we personally get to know people from different cultures, especially if we are working toward a common goal, we begin to learn from one another and grow in love. If you have been on a mission trip in another country before, you may have come back with a glimpse of how that culture worships differently, prays differently, or emphasizes different aspects of God. We express gratitude for having the opportunity to experience this difference, but then we return to our homogeneous worship environments without giving it a second thought. It's as if we don't realize that we could get that here, in our own backyards! What if we were to put ourselves in situations more frequently—in our home countries—where we could learn from Christians who are different than us? Imagine just how much our faith could expand if we opened our hearts and our minds to it! Just as I learned when I moved from Laredo to Austin, every culture has strengths and weaknesses in their worship of God, different understandings of Scripture, and varied expressions of ministry. We have so much to learn from one another.

Diversity Helps Us See God

The journey starts with acknowledging the diversity surrounding our churches and welcoming diversity into our churches, but it does not end there. We must learn to celebrate diversity as a church. There is richness in being in relationship with people different than ourselves. Diversity helps complete a visual manifestation of the creative revelation of God.

Some people believe that ethnicity is a man-made construct and not from God; however, ethnic and cultural differences are actually a gift from God by design. We consistently see the term *ethnos* (Greek for "ethnic" and "ethnicity") in the Bible to describe the different people groups and nations representing different languages and cultures. Remember that in Acts 17:26 (ESV), Paul states that God "made from one man every nation of mankind to live on all the face of the earth." We know that God created us in his image (Genesis 1:26-27); therefore, the diversity of his creation reflects the diversity that characterizes his own nature.[2]

Appreciating the beauty of someone's culture and perspective is not just something we should do from afar. We need to open ourselves up to learn from one another and be enriched by a different approach to life and faith, and this can only be done in mutual relationship. If we want to be on mission with God, we will need some cultural humility, meaning we must stop thinking that only our culture, our way, is best.

Accommodation, Not Assimilation

When we believe our approaches to church are the only way, then we expect different kinds of people to adapt to us and become like us. This will never work in the body of Christ. In *Leading a Healthy Multi-Ethnic Church*, Mark DeYmaz explains why a "healthy multiethnic church will be established not by assimilation but rather by accommodation." While the word *assimilate* means to eliminate or minimize differences, the word *accommodate* means "to adjust actions in response to somebody's needs."[3] Giving up our privilege is one of the hardest things we will do, but when we begin to accommodate other people and truly appreciate the beauty of the culture they express, we see enormous benefits.

When you worship, study the Bible, or do ministry with people of different ethnicities, you'll begin to notice how we all manifest different facets of God's nature and articulate them with a different passion. Let me give you an example from my Latino/a culture. We are an extremely relational people known for our collective/family orientation. We place a lot of importance on building community and on personal connections in our interactions. When a group of Latinos come together for a ministry meeting, it's common for the agenda to start late and for the meeting to last longer than planned. Why is that? Because we spend so much time connecting on a personal level, sharing updates about our families, and sharing prayer requests. (Obviously, this is not always true in every situation, but I've found it to be exceedingly accurate in my experience.) A friend once told me a story about a young, white man who got involved in a Latino ministry. Since he came from a time- and task-oriented culture, at first he was frustrated with how long it took the group to get to the point in their meetings! If only they would just skip over all of the conversation and jump right to the agenda, they could be so much more efficient, he thought. But as time went on, the man came to see the benefits of their approach. He began to notice that decisions were made faster after the personal connections had been made, as opposed to meetings where this wasn't prioritized and decisions seemed to take longer. Not only did he learn to see the value, but he also learned to love and appreciate their cultural approach, even if it was different than his.

Remember: God made us all in his image, and there is beauty in his design. When we're interacting with cultures that are more relational than what we prefer, perhaps we are getting a glimpse into God's longing to have a deep, personal connection with us. It truly is beautiful when we get to experience vicariously the varying qualities of God through our brothers and sisters in Christ.

When Dennis and Joy, who are white, decided to join an African American church, the first thing they discovered was that the worship was very different than what they were used to. It was loud, repetitive, and went on for so long that they had to move to a "dead spot" in the sanctuary so that they could make it through the worship set. It took a while for them to get used to this new style of worship, but eventually they came to appreciate the beauty in how their black brothers and sisters worshiped the Lord. It wasn't a programmed, clear start and finish, going-through-the-motions kind of way. The repetition and call-and-response elements made it easy to participate. There was space for the Holy Spirit to speak since they weren't in a rush to move on to the next thing. It was lively, and the Spirit of God was visible. Years later, Dennis and Joy found themselves visiting a white church. After the worship ended, Joy remarked to Dennis, "Well, that worship was boring. But at least it was short!" They had opened up their hearts to a different way of doing church, and they came to love and value the differences.

Perhaps one of the best learning opportunities available in a diverse church setting is studying the Bible with people of different backgrounds and cultures. Zach Szmara is a white pastor of a multiethnic church called the Bridge Community Wesleyan Church in Logansport, Indiana. He has had a front-row seat in experiencing the richness of different cultures. Specifically, it has enriched his understanding of the Bible. After growing up listening to Bible stories from the same perspective, he realized as an adult just how much his biblical interpretation has been influenced by white, Western men. He'll never forget the moment he heard an interpretation of John 4 from a woman who had been sexually exploited in her past. To see this woman's reaction to Jesus offering the Samaritan woman water, and elevating her instead of abusing her, opened Pastor Zach's eyes to the Scripture in a way he had never seen. The more time he has spent around marginalized people, the more he realizes that they see things in the Bible that he completely misses—and his teaching and preaching has improved because of it. As Christians, we are all rooted in seeing things from one perspective. When we open ourselves up to different cultures and perspectives, we will inevitably see more of God.

As an ethnic minority who has spent a lot of time in both minority- and majority-culture Christian contexts, I have found that taking the posture of a cultural explorer is of great value.

When I encounter a culture that is different than mine, I look for similar cultural connections in order to create a tangible sense of unity, as well as take note of differences and ask myself what those characteristics teach me about God. Leaning into our connections, coupled with our common faith, lowers our sense of isolation and makes our ministry together more effective. I admit, this requires a bit of cultural literacy that increases with experience, but I implore you to not be intimidated, even if you are just starting on the journey. If we all enter in with a humble posture and lots of grace, there is so much we can learn from one another.

The Beauty of Teamwork

Part of my dream is to see Christians learn how to harness the power of diversity within the church. Fritz Dale, one of my mentors in my denomination, constantly hammered into me the value of teamwork amidst diversity. We had the leaders of different ministries (women's, students', ethnic minority, church planting) come together on our denominational leadership team for the specific purpose of building synergy. Those who know me know how much of a basketball fan I am, especially for my home team, the San Antonio Spurs. I have learned that I am not just biased; San Antonio really is where some of the best basketball is played. Sports commentators have long spoken about how the team's diverse culture, team synergy, and commitment to the purity of the game—while avoiding the flair seen in other popular NBA teams—has made them so successful.

"Beautiful basketball" is a phrase that many sports writers have used to describe the way the Spurs play together as a team.[4] Here are some of the reasons why:

1. The Spurs not only have a diversity of personalities and styles of playing, but they also have a diversity of ethnicities

represented. In fact, they have had the most international players of any other NBA team. This international dynamic has helped them to be more team oriented, as opposed to individual centric.

2. Everyone on the court is equal. This quality starts with their coach, Gregg Popovich, who does not allow for any ball hogs. Popovich will call out the superstar for criticism as quickly as the rookie. The players respect each other. You rarely see them screaming at each other, even if a mistake is made during the game.

3. They emphasize the fundamentals of the game, such as ball movement, which is indicative of good teamwork. They are all focused on the same goal—putting more points on the board than the other team. In fact, the essence of their victory comes with their unselfish passing of the ball around in such a way that opposing teams can't defend against it. That kind of synergy does not happen by practicing a lot or having the best players. Their greatness comes from playing for each other. It comes from knowing their differences and yet applying those differences to the greater goal.

Beautiful Ministry

In general, the church over the years has not played beautiful ministry. We have been more characterized by individualistic approaches, lack of unity, focusing on the wrong things, and being satisfied with a few marquee leaders that attract a crowd. If we are to be effective in ministry, we need to hold three things in equal tension:

1. God's creation of diversity is good! If we want to win, we must quit running from it; we must embrace it and see it as his gift to reach the nations among us.

2. We need to play fundamentals. We need to make sure those fundamentals are not ethnocentric but bibliocentric.
3. We all, from superstars to rookies, need to hold the values of mutual respect, love for team members as God's gift to the team, and winning for the glory of God.

When I hear stories about churches like New Life and Bridge Community, I get the sense they are engaged in beautiful ministry. It doesn't happen from one day to the next; there is a sequence that takes time to unfold. It starts with acknowledging the diversity surrounding our churches, then welcoming diversity into the church, then celebrating diversity as a church, then harnessing the power of diversity within the church, and finally, unleashing a diverse church into the wider world.

A Testimony to the World

I opened this chapter with the story of New Life Church in Aurora, Colorado, because they are a fantastic example of a church that embraced the beauty of the changing community around them. A few years after they made the shift to a multiethnic community, they began hosting an event called Taste of the Nations that draws thousands of people every year. The celebration was a vision of taking the church outside the walls, reaching the community, and celebrating the unique cultures represented in their congregations. They have music, food, dancing, and brief testimonies from church members. They try to be sensitive to cultural differences; for example, the amazing Korean pork BBQ is at one end of the buffet, and their Arabic halal booth is at the other! Not only has it been a fun event to host, but it has also been a powerful testimony for Christ in the city of Aurora. City leaders, such as congresspeople, fire fighters, and the police chief, have begun attending the event and have even been prayed over. Many sitting in their services met Christ through this event. It's rare to see ethnicities and cultures coming together in such a way, so the community started to take notice. There have been multiple instances in which the city government has called upon the church's leadership to provide insight into ethnic and cultural dynamics in the city.

To this I say—what a marvelous testimony for Christ's love! In John 13:35 (NIV), Jesus says, "By this everyone will know that you are my disciples, if you love one another." If we truly want people to know that we are Jesus' disciples, we will strive to love one another in ways that the world is not used to witnessing.

We must acknowledge, however, that the process can be costly. Loving people from different cultures is about more than just appreciating their food, music, language, and interpretation of Scripture. It's not always a party. The rubber meeting the road comes when we start to feel safe enough with one another to share our pain. The closer we come to one another, the more potential there is for conflict born of our differences to emerge. How will we respond when it does? Will we peace out with a dismissive wave, or will we lean in with empathy?

REFLECTION

Consecrating Prayer: Lord, please help me see the beauty in all ethnicities and cultures, as they were created by you, and bring people into my life who will expose me to new perspectives.

Head Work: Think about your own ethnic or cultural background. Even if you are a white American who is generations removed from an immigration experience, you still have a culture! What ideals, values, and traditions does your family celebrate? What do you find beautiful about your culture?

Heart Work: Reflect on this hymn about ethnic diversity and unity, written by John Oxenham, 1852–1941.

In Christ there is no east or west,
In him no south or north,
But one great fellowship of love
Throughout the whole wide earth.

In him shall true hearts everywhere
Their high communion find,
His service is the golden cord
Close-binding humankind.

Join hands, united in the faith,
Whate'er your race may be!
Who serves my Father as a son
Is surely kin to me.

In Christ now meet both east and west,
In him meet south and north,
All Christ-like souls are one in him,
Throughout the whole wide earth.

Hands Work: Congregate with your family around the kitchen table and begin writing down aspects of different cultures that you find beautiful. (Think about what you have learned from being around people of other ethnicities, socioeconomic backgrounds, or generations.) Write each insight on a 3 x 5 notecard. Do this exercise every Friday night until you have one hundred cards in your stack.

RESOURCES

- Visit captivatinghistory.com to learn more about a series of history ebooks that educate readers on different people groups, countries, movements, and more.

- Book Suggestions: *The Colors of Culture* by MelindaJoy Mingo; *Misreading Scripture with Western Eyes* by E. Randolph Richards and Brandon J. O'Brien; *Living in Color* by Randy Woodley
- Bible Study Suggestion: *Ethnic Identity: Bringing Your Full Self to God* by Steve Tamayo

CHAPTER 6

Entering into the Pain
of the Marginalized

If one part suffers, every part suffers with it.

1 CORINTHIANS 12:26, NIV

I DO NOT BELIEVE I would be where I am today if it weren't for Bill Hamel, the EFCA's former president. When I was young and very early on in my ministry career, Bill took a gamble on me—a strange Mexican American from Laredo, Texas. Bill was the master of extending ministry beyond himself. On my first trip to the EFCA National Office in Minneapolis, I felt like an outsider. During our meeting, I sat as far away from everybody as I could. But Bill made me get up and sit between him and the outgoing president. In subsequent years, he kept putting me on different national boards; I later realized that he was preparing me for working for him. I eventually learned what a big heart he had for equipping ethnic minority and immigrant leaders. Ironically, Bill grew up in Wisconsin, where a few of his family members were sympathetic to some of the views of the Ku Klux Klan in the area. As a young man, anti-Catholic, anti-black, and anti-immigrant sentiments were not uncommon in his world. Once he grew up and left home, he attended Wheaton College in Illinois, where he played football. Some of his fellow linemen were African American, and he began to see firsthand the hurt and the pain they experienced on a daily basis. Once again, we see contact theory and the power of proximity in action. He began to get to know people of color for the first time and grow in love for the marginalized. It was then that he started on a journey that would continue until his death.

After I was hired to work for him in 2006, together we created several programs that have become part of the EFCA's fabric to love and serve the marginalized. He mentored me, protected me when I was vulnerable (since at the time our programs were controversial), and advised me against things when he felt the need, but ultimately allowed me to pursue what I felt called to. He awed me with his trust. When the nation went through major financial stress in 2008, the EFCA had to reduce the staff, but Bill would not allow the ethnic minority leaders to be let go. Because of the leadership's efforts, the EFCA increased from 7 percent diversity in 2000 to 23 percent in 2019. Other denominations have also done a great job at increasing diversity, such as the Assemblies of God, the Free Methodist Church, the Evangelical Covenant Church, and the Christian and Missionary Alliance.

Bill is an example of a white majority-culture leader who entered into relationship with ethnic minority leaders and allowed himself to feel their pain. But it didn't stop there. He saw the injustice at play and figured out ways to use his privilege and leadership position to empower the marginalized and create programs that work to bring justice.

Chapter 5 was all about appreciating the beauty and diversity of God's people, but we cannot stop there. Truly loving the marginalized community means not only appreciating the beauty of their culture but also understanding the pain and injustices they endure. Entering into pain with our brothers and sisters in Christ is what will help us grow in love for the New Samaria.

What Is Love?

Scripture is very clear about what it looks like, practically speaking, to love our neighbor. In 1 John 3:16-18 (NIV), we read: "This is how we know what love is: Jesus Christ laid down his life for us. And we ought to lay down our lives for our brothers and sisters. If anyone has material possessions and sees a brother or sister in need but has no pity on them, how can the love of God be in that person? Dear children, let us not love with words or speech but with actions and in truth."

I think about this Scripture often. There is no room for misunderstanding. We cannot claim to love the poor, the marginalized, and the strangers among us if we have no empathy for them and leave them in need. It calls out those who have "material possessions," but I would also include those who possess privilege in our society—especially those who are in the ethnic and cultural majority—whether financially wealthy or not. This is not a calling only for specific people who are passionate about "these kinds of things." It is a mandate from God given to us because of the fact that God laid down his life, and we ought to do the same for others.

We see a similar call in Galatians 6:2-3 (NIV), which reads, "Carry each other's burdens, and in this way you will fulfill the law of Christ. If anyone thinks they are something when they are not, they deceive themselves." And in 1 Corinthians 12:26 (NIV): "If one part suffers, every part suffers with it." If we are truly seeking to be a united body of Christ, then we should not and cannot go on without feeling one another's suffering.

Unfortunately for the empowered majority, having privilege and resources and comfort tends to insulate us from pain and need. Sometimes we have the luxury of ignoring the pain of others, especially if we're not in relationship with one another regularly. That's not to say that those in power and privilege don't experience pain. We all know that poverty can impact anyone, and people of any color and ethnicity can fall on hard times. But we must remember that our institutions tend to be designed to better support the needs of dominant cultures. It is harder for some to dig themselves out or "pull themselves up by their bootstraps," as the saying goes. The pain people of color and immigrants experience is different because of the structural biases at play, and we must recognize the steep challenges and barriers they face. For example, they may not be able to connect with school, medical, or social services because of language, transportation, or even trust issues with the providers of services.

Examples of What Churches Can Do

In chapter 4, I started telling the story of Shoreline Community Church in Santa Barbara, California, which experienced a significant demographic change in their neighborhood, leading them to begin ministering to their immigrant neighbors. When the church leaders decided to try to start a children's ministry, they singled out a church member named Diane Martinez, who was an early childhood teacher. She and her husband had moved into the neighborhood because her husband had bought a home there many years ago. She never planned on doing ministry among immigrants, but there she was right in the middle of the largest and densest Latino immigrant population in Santa Barbara. She recounts, "Even though my last name is Martinez, I spoke almost no Spanish at the time. My background was so different than theirs. I remember feeling so out of place."

Aware of her training as an early childhood educator, the church leaders asked Diane if she would temporarily lead their children's ministry, and she agreed. A bilingual, retired missionary began to take her with him into the neighborhoods, meeting kids and their families. Little by little, God began to transform Diane's heart. Her feelings of discomfort toward a community different than what she was accustomed to began to change once she got to know them personally. Many of the parents worked in the hospitality industry and had odd hours, so the church opened their doors to the neighborhood kids who wanted to spend time there when their parents weren't home. For five years the church poured into these kids, and as they got to know their families, they saw the injustices and pain they were experiencing from trying to make their way in this new country. They struggled with exhausting days of work and lack of childcare, and then, too often, they experienced or witnessed frequent deportations that were splitting families apart. Diane began to ache for them. The needs were endless, and she couldn't sit back and do nothing.

A postcard arrived in the mail from her denomination describing a ministry called Immigrant Hope, which equips churches to provide trained guidance on permanent residency and citizenship embedded in Christian caring. Diane just knew that this was the ministry that could best meet the practical needs and address the pain of her community.

So in 2012, despite fears and some opposition, Shoreline Community Church took the first steps toward becoming an Immigrant Hope site, hoping to serve and engage with their neighbors. Diane began training in immigration law and processes. An anonymous donation funded a salary so she could be full time.

Some people in the church suspected that Immigrant Hope was doing something illegal in trying to help immigrants with their immigration status. The leaders found themselves having to address that misconception head on, assuring church members that Immigrant Hope partnered with the US government and wasn't helping immigrants skirt the law. People who felt hesitant at first began to come around when they saw the practical impact the ministry was having. Over the years they have had contact with many hundreds of immigrants in a fifty-mile radius. The controversy raised awareness in the church of the growing immigrant presence and the opportunity to love their neighbors as themselves. The once-reluctant Diane would not trade anything for the joy of serving God in Samerica.

Immigrant Hope, the ministry highlighted in the story above, is the ministry that Bill Hamel and I started together when I worked under him at the EFCA. He knew very well my heart for the marginalized—specifically immigrants. I truly believe that this is one of the major areas where God is at work in this country. As I described in chapter 2, the demographics in our country are changing rapidly. Studies show that 55 percent of our growth is a direct result of immigrants and their American-born children. By 2065, nearly 20 percent of people in the country will have been born outside of American borders.[1] This phenomenon is not unique to America; it is happening all over the world. If we as a church are not reaching immigrants where they are at, in all the messiness of their circumstances, then we are missing out on a spectacular missional opportunity to love and reach our neighbors.

I love this quote from Wayne Gretzky, who has been called the greatest hockey player in the history of the NHL: "A good hockey player plays where the puck is. A great hockey player plays where the puck is going to be."[2] As Christians, we need to keep our eyes on where the church is going, not where the church has been.

But reaching immigrants is not the only way. There are many examples of wonderful churches that are reaching marginalized communities and seeking justice for their neighbors. I wish I could tell every story I have, but those would fill a book of its own. Let me share two more examples with the hope of inspiring you to think outside the box.

Looking Ahead to Minister

At Hilltop Urban Church in Wichita, Kansas, ministry to their neighbors began revealing the prevalence of domestic violence in their community. In caring for people and sharing the love of Christ with them, they couldn't ignore the pain that many women and children were experiencing at home. One man in particular, Dennis Hesselbarth, was moved to action by the stories he heard. In doing his research, he found out that the local city ordinance required women to file charges against their partners before the police would step in. This, he discovered, was very hard to do, as many of the women believed it was their fault or were scared to make the first move. So he joined an effort to change the city ordinance so that police could arrest an abuser when evidence was clear, not requiring the women to file first. This change made a world of difference. As the church counseled women and taught them what the Bible says is true—that they have dignity and worth and value—they could also provide tangible advice on what steps to take to keep their families safe. Many of us see unjust situations around us and think there is nothing we can do, but oftentimes there are things we can do. The first step is opening our eyes to the pain and injustice and then moving to action.

Here's yet another example. In chapter 5, I told the story about New Life Church in Aurora, Colorado, that began hosting the Taste of the Nations event as a way of celebrating the beauty of the cultures represented in their church. But they didn't stop there. As they got to know the stories of the people in their neighborhood, they began hosting conferences about immigration and refugee reform, as well as addressing the problem of racism in our country. The horror of George Floyd's death prompted the church to repent of the sin of racism and address the issue head on. One Sunday the African American pastor, the Latino pastor, and the Filipino pastor got up together and spoke from the pulpit about their experiences with racism. They expounded on Scripture that would help everyone think biblically about these issues. One of their church members, a white man who works for the police force, felt moved to address the church on a Sunday morning. He offered a heartfelt apology on behalf of all police. This unexpected gesture of overt humility made a big impact in building trust and reconciliation between the majority- and minority-culture congregants.

Pastor Jeff Noble will tell you that being a multicultural and justice-oriented community has not been easy. Like roommates who are vastly different, sometimes their approaches to life and faith drive one another crazy. But the single biggest key has been viewing themselves as one body. When you begin to live life with other people, their pain becomes your pain, and it's impossible to ignore it. This is the beauty of the Kingdom of God.

Four Basic Principles

My goal for this chapter was to illustrate the things we as a church should be doing as we enter into the pain of the marginalized. To be clear, I will summarize them here:

1. We must *acknowledge* that we are all made in God's image and are endowed with different positional and innate privilege. This is neither good or bad. Rather than deny our privilege, we must leverage it to further his Kingdom purposes.

2. We must *engage* in efforts as a church to practically care for the needs and pain of our neighbors and work to advocate for righteous treatment for all people made in God's image.

3. We must *repudiate* the notion that God's mission can be accomplished by guarding the status quo without robust biblical cultural engagement. Our mission as Christians

should involve actively seeking change through the systems of our society that can help bring justice to the least of these.

4. We must *empower* the marginalized by investing in their leadership development, supporting their initiatives, and resourcing them to reach their communities. This group will soon be leading the church in matters of missional strategy, and now is the time for us to intentionally seek their counsel.

I'm afraid the problem with the American church is that our vision is too small. We have become too comfortable. Jesus came to revolutionize the world. He lent fresh eyes to what the Jews already knew, that we are created in the image of God, but he included everyone—the poor, the sick, the sinful, the marginalized, even the Roman oppressors. The status quo was such a strong wind that the disciples couldn't see the need to reach Samaria.

This really begs the question: Will we as the church open our eyes and hearts to see and love the marginalized in our midst? Will we work for justice for the vulnerable? I believe Paul would tell us:

Awake, you who sleep,
Arise from the dead,
And Christ will give you light.
EPHESIANS 5:14

We must wake up and embrace the pain that exists all around us. Some would say that this is an opportunity to recapture our humanity. That may very well be, but that would not be enough for me. I want to see transformation. This is our opportunity to join God where he is at work in the next rise of Christianity! The journey is not easy, but it will be worth it.

REFLECTION

Consecrating Prayer: Lord, we are all passing through this world. Help me see myself as your ambassador who is called to love, help, and heal those you bring across my path. Lord, expand my heart to be a burden bearer as you were and are for me.

Head Work: Think of a time when you saw a person in pain or in need and helped them. Also think about a time you saw someone in pain or in need and did not help them. What was the difference between the two situations? Were there internal or external factors affecting whether or not you chose to help?

Heart Work: Lord, help me be pricked by your Holy Spirit when I am lacking empathy or compassion for people in need. Reflect on that.

Hands Work: Tonight, pick up the local newspaper and scan for stories of injustice happening in your community—stories about racism, sexism, abuse, sex trafficking, poverty. Who are the people being affected by injustice? Ask God to open your eyes to what you have learned to ignore. Pray and do what the Spirit pricks your heart to do.

RESOURCES

- Book Suggestions: *The New Jim Crow* by Michelle Alexander; *Rediscipling the White Church* by David W. Swanson; *Race and Place* by David Leong
- Other Resources: "The Stories of Migrants Risking Everything for a Better Life" by Haley Sweetland Edwards (https://www.time.com/longform/migrants/); "The Danger of a Single Story" by Chimamanda Ngozi Adichie (https://www.teds.com/talks/ chimamanda_ngozi _adichie_the_danger_of_a_single_story?language=en)

reach the new samaria

CHAPTER 7

Strategy Transformation

Behold, I will do a new thing,
Now it shall spring forth;
Shall you not know it?
I will even make a road in the wilderness
And rivers in the desert.

ISAIAH 43:19

THE CONCEPT OF REACHING THE LOST is nothing new to the evangelical movement. Anyone raised in Christian culture has undoubtedly internalized the importance of sharing our faith with nonbelievers. In fact, some of you reading this book might be thinking, *Finally, the section I've been waiting for!* That's because, for many Christians, the vulnerable and marginalized populations among us are approached as a project—they are the people who need saving, we must be the ones to save them, so please, tell us what we need to do!

There are several problems with this mindset. First, we begin to view ourselves in a hierarchy in which those in the majority-culture population are better or more valuable than the poor and the marginalized. This often leads to a savior mentality, in which we forget that Jesus is the one who does the saving, not us. Second, many Christians have forgotten that while reaching the vulnerable is a mandate from God, it cannot be done in the absence of love and respect. Third, we falsely assume that we are the only ones coming to the table with something to offer, when in reality we have so much to learn.

My goal for this section is to call the church back to an evangelistic approach that focuses less on excellence, numbers, size of buildings, and large budgets, and more on what it takes to reach the end goal: *transformation*. And I don't just mean the personal and individual transformation we experience when we encounter Jesus; while that is part of it, we need to also be seeking transformation in our communities that flows out of being a church that sees and loves our neighbors, as Jesus commanded us.

The Great Commission and Great Compassion

I graduated from UT Austin with postgraduate degrees in social work and community development. After a couple of years working as a social worker, I went to Dallas Theological Seminary, which is known to be one of the most conservative seminaries in the nation. The contrast between the two experiences was like the convergence of the warm waters of the Rio Grande and the cold waters of the Red River in North Dakota.

I wish I had a dollar for each time I've been asked this question: "How could you go to such a liberal school and get a liberal degree like social work and then attend Dallas Theological Seminary and not go crazy?"

It's the same as all of life: Eat the fish and spit out the bones.

It's rare to find Christian institutions that can hold the Great Commission and Great Commandment together in proper tension. It has been obvious to me ever since my time at DTS that there is an imbalance in the evangelical church. Some people and churches lean toward social concern, such as food banks, justice issues, or community development. Other people and churches focus on teaching the Bible, evangelistic efforts, and developing leaders. Some churches not only lean one way, but they also disparage the other as liberal or fundamentalist. Rare is the church that understands the need for both. Some large churches seem to do both because of their size, even if by accident. But that is not enough. What we all really need is an intentional plan.

I came up with a simple equation I use regularly to remind myself and others of God's marching orders. I call it the GC3:

THE GREAT COMMISSION AND GREAT COMMANDMENT BUILD GREAT COMMUNITY.

A Perfect Model

One must look no further than the New Testament to see Jesus as the social worker and lover of people—passionate to feed, heal, and bind up the wounded. Yet the same Jesus would sit them down and preach the most profound and theological teaching. Same guy, same God. He didn't change his hat and speak from a different perspective. Jesus was modeling two Great Commandments he set out for the disciples: the Great Commandment and the Great Commission. For Jesus, there was perfect harmony in this simple effort.

The Great Commandment comes out of Matthew 22:36-40 (NIV), where Jesus tells us to "love the Lord your God with all your heart and with all your soul and with all your mind. . . . [And] love your neighbor as yourself." I would add John 13:34-35 (NIV), in which Jesus said, "As I have loved you, so you must love one another. By this everyone will know that you are my disciples, if you love one another." This is the engine that starts the process of transformation. Jesus was undoubtedly a good teacher, but what initially attracted people to him was his concern for their well-being. He fed, healed, and loved them. I cannot emphasize enough—we must never minimize this important ministry that was predicted in Isaiah 61.[1] This is why I focused part 2 of the book on it. However, some people/churches/organizations get so good at the work of pursuing biblical justice that they fail to hold it in proper tension with the mandate to make disciples.

The Great Commission (Matthew 28:19-20) picks up where the Great Commandment left off. Jesus didn't come just to feed people. He came to make disciples who make disciples (Matthew 4:19) and die so that we may have life to the full (John 10:10). The problem with many of our churches is that the Great Commission is often divorced from the Great Commandment. We become so preoccupied with evangelism/discipleship that we forget to love our neighbors as ourselves. Our churches can become so preoccupied with executing outreach programs and sermons in an attempt to get people into heaven, but without love, we risk slipping into a Pharisaism that Jesus warned his disciples about.[2] There is value in having a tension between the Great Commission and the Great Commandment, as every person has different passions and spiritual giftings, and every church is made up of a mix of people and personalities. What we do *not* want is for Christians to assume that everyone should share our unique gifts and passions, something that Larry Osborne in his book *Accidental Pharisees* refers to as "gift projection."[3] But as Christian leaders we must do our best to uphold both of Jesus' mandates in tandem. Both are essential to the heart of the Lord.

Adaptive Leadership

Resetting the church does not mean looking for a new mission or mandate of love. It means reimagining how we live it out in our day. When the disciples went on mission, they walked. We have adapted by flying. The disciples carried parchment. Now we have printed Bibles and digital versions. We need to make another paradigm leap where we can integrate the Great Commission with the Great Commandment by engaging with all kinds of people who have all kinds of feathers who can flock together.

Communion Chapel was a church in decline in a part of San Antonio that was transitioning demographically. They had dwindled to fewer than fifty people. They were a church that had lost its missional focus and needed some recalibration. The leaders knew they needed a pastor who was passionate about both the Great Commandment and the Great Commission, as their community was in need. They hired Roderick Barns, an African American pastor who lived and breathed the GC3. His secret sauce was helping the church walk out the synergy of the two great mandates of love and life-on-life disciplemaking. They began asking how they could tangibly love their neighbors. One way was to build relationships with families at several low-income apartment complexes in the area. They saw that many of the children needed support after school, so church members began volunteering to help children do homework at the apartment building. They also began preparing meals for the families and offering to pray with them. As relationships started developing, many of the families began attending church. They have turned themselves around and become a diverse and flourishing community.

The people at Communion Chapel were not all churchified. All were not in "Sunday best." They were from all walks of life. The interesting thing was that even in their diversity, they were united. They found their sweet spot in this tension between the Great Commission and the Great Commandment and began experiencing transformation.

Addressing the Blind Spots on Both Sides

Since most of us tend to lean one way or another, I will address the blind spots that exist on both sides. If you are someone who has put more emphasis on the Great Commission, whether intentionally or not, and have been a bit too passive in loving those who are vulnerable, my question for you is: What is stopping you from going all in? If we have placed our theological footing well, are we not the most well-equipped people to love our neighbors? I believe so. Unfortunately, too many churches and Christian leaders have been silent or passive about social problems facing our communities. This silence and passivity ultimately equates to indifference; thus, many people think the church doesn't have anything to say about these issues. I believe this has been a failure of the church, and if we don't change our ways, one of the repercussions (among many) will be the continual exodus of younger generations from the faith. It is essential for us to listen to the concerns of younger leaders, since they clearly have a stake in the future outcome.

Now, if you are someone who has leaned into the Great Commandment and placed less emphasis on the Great Commission, my exhortation for you is this: Do not forget the power of the gospel. We must acknowledge that human efforts at compassion, apart from a gospel focus, eventually go wayward. This is why we must seek compassion and justice with a gospel focus, as there is no ultimate justice apart from Jesus. While the poor were an important focus of Jesus' ministry on earth, the latter part of Matthew 26:11 intimates another priority, namely about the Lord and his work. Jesus said, "The poor you will always have with you, but you will not always have me" (Matthew 26:11, NIV). There is no end to the hurt in this world. Helping the poor is a mark of a disciple, but not at the expense of making disciples. Truly, if done right, preaching and serving are almost seamless. When the disciples were first sent out to practice this ministry, Jesus told them to proclaim the

Good News and "heal the sick, cleanse the lepers, raise the dead, cast out demons" (Matthew 10:7-8). If we really want the gospel to penetrate the culture of our community, we must speak Good News *and* practice Good News at the same time.

The True Litmus Test

When I refer to the "Great Transformed Community," I am referring to the church, the church's place within its city, and the testimony among the people who see its good work (Acts 2:47; 5:13-14). This is our true litmus test. The church was never meant to be an island protected by moats and drawbridges. Ours is a building without walls—open for all to come in. We have got to quit writing manuals and implementing programs that practice marching our soldiers within the fortress without the intention of going to war. If we are not seeing transformation, we really need to question if our expressions of the Great Commission and of the Great Commandment are bound in our personality or in the power of the Holy Spirit.

• • •

After Pastor Charles Wilson and his wife dropped off their son Kyree at college in Lynchburg, Virginia, they stopped for ice cream in a city called Roanoke. Hits Ice Cream was a local mom-and-pop spot next to a beautiful greenway and at the foot of Mill Mountain. It was on that mountain overlooking the entire valley that the Lord began to call them into church planting in Roanoke. It took a few years to understand the challenging context they were being invited into. Redlining practices and urban renewal contributed to the many challenges in the city. They decided to start their ministry along the border of the city's four sections, on the city's northwest side. It is predominantly African American and known for high levels of poverty, gun violence, and drug activity. As Pastor Charles began to build relationships, he learned that many of their neighbors were hesitant about the church. Unfortunately, this community had seen many churches turn their focus primarily inward. Later, when they bought an old, abandoned church building to renovate, they discovered a Jacuzzi-style bathtub in what used to be the senior pastor's office! It was no wonder that some community members questioned their motives.

After a while, Pastor Charles began to gain their trust. Their physical location in the heart of the northwest side near downtown has allowed them to gain credibility from a diverse group of people from around the city. Their church has become known as an outwardly focused, diverse community that loves God, loves their neighbors, and makes disciples. Not only do they care about winning souls for Christ, but they also care about the flourishing of their city. They partner with their police department and their local Feeding America food bank. Pastor Charles served on the committee that developed the city's 2040 strategic plan, and he was also appointed by city council to serve on the neighborhood services committee. And during the 2020 global pandemic, the Hill Church worked directly with their local state representative to distribute twenty thousand masks and hand sanitizer to the most vulnerable in Roanoke.

I like to refer to the Great Commission and the Great Commandment as irreducible elements of our faith, as they cannot be simplified or reinvented. The Hill Church is an example of how we need to refresh our expression and focus of these elements. If we are going to succeed at reaching the New Samaria, we need an accountability between the two. The Great Commission is what we need to be doing, but the Great Commandment is how we need to do it. We can't take one and leave the other.

When we can match our good stand on orthodoxy with

sacrificial compassion and justice, when we can see the strangers among us as people made in the image of God, when we can see the gospel opportunities outside of our church walls, then our church will truly be a transformational movement.

REFLECTION

Consecrating Prayer: Lord, help us to be a church that places equal importance on the Great Commission and the Great Commandment, understanding that both are necessary to see transformation.

Head Work: How have you approached the Great Commission and the Great Commandment in your faith journey? Have you leaned into one more than the other? Why?

Heart Work: Is there any fear, doubt, weariness, or resentment in your heart that keeps you from living out either of God's mandates in your day-to-day life? Stop here and give those to the Lord.

Hands Work: Commit to sharing the Good News of the gospel with one person this week, but do it after meeting a practical need in their life. If you are not regularly serving people who are in need, find a ministry or organization where you could volunteer.

RESOURCES

- Find opportunities near you at volunteermatch.org.
- Explore the free and simple online evangelism training at evantell.org.
- Book Suggestions: *Reimagining Evangelism* by Rick Richardson; *Great Commission, Great Compassion* by Paul Borthwick

CHAPTER 8

Making Disciples

*And the things that you have heard from me
among many witnesses, commit these to faithful
men who will be able to teach others also.*

2 TIMOTHY 2:2

WHEN I GOT MY FIRST EMAIL ADDRESS in 1987, it was makedisciples@ aol.com. I was a Jesus freak and wanted everyone to know it. As soon as I came to know the Lord, I had a huge passion for becoming a disciple and making disciples—and I attribute this to the fact that I became a Christian through the ministry of The Navigators. At the University of Texas, they were the only campus ministry that seriously focused on disciplemaking (at least that's what we thought). In fact, we joke that back then The Navigators were called the "never-daters." The male and female ministries generally worked independently and only connected a few times throughout the year. This part of the Navigator culture was very difficult for me because, being a Latino, I wanted to hug everybody, especially my Navigator sisters! I would have also hugged my Navigator brothers, but I had to tame these aspects of my culture because I was already too strange anyway. I could try my best to be a good Navigator, but I didn't know how to be a bad Latino.

I was one of the only ethnic minorities in an almost entirely white campus ministry, and my peculiarities made me feel like I was broken or a bit crazy. Perhaps some of it was just my perception, but it was obvious I didn't have the same interests, taste, jokes, music, or common vocabulary as the other students. I was different, and it grated on my cultural senses. One semester, Mark Lewis, the guy who led our discipleship group of six, decided that we should travel to each other's houses to do work projects. So we traveled to Laredo on Friday night. On Saturday morning my mother made us breakfast tacos, which is a customary breakfast in South Texas. She had bowls of chorizo with eggs, beans with cheese, chicharrones, potatoes with egg, and homemade flour tortillas. One of the students wasn't so sure about the strange food, so he asked my mother if we had any peanut butter to put in the tortilla. I don't remember if we had peanut butter, but my brothers ribbed me mercilessly over that for years. In all, it was a successful trip, because my mom's fear of hippies went down about 75 percent.

Even though my time with The Navigators had its challenges due to the culture shock I experienced, I would not trade it for anything. We were all young and doing the best we could to walk with the Lord, and experiencing the culture clashes taught us all valuable lessons about ministry. Most of all, The Navigators instilled in me tools for cross-cultural discipleship that I've carried with me my whole life.

The Problem Facing the Church

The denomination I work for did an internal survey among pastors to ask: What makes a disciple? The top answers from pastors were

- Going to church
- Listening to sermons and podcasts
- Giving money to the church
- Being a missionary

These answers came as a surprise to me. While all of these things are good, they are not what make us disciples. The machine of the church in our day has confused the matter of what it means to be a disciple. One of the biggest problems facing the church is that not all of our pastors have ever truly been discipled either! If church leaders are confused about this, I wouldn't expect lay Christians to have much more insight.

Discipleship is about becoming transformed into the image of Christ. It is progressive, not instantaneous. It is not about faith as much as faithfulness and obedience. As committed disciples, we must choose to put our faith in Christ alone, and then "work out"[1] the sanctification process of taking up our cross daily to follow him (Matthew 16:24-26). It is a daily challenge, and it cannot be done alone. Sinning and failing do not disqualify us; ask Peter, who denied our Lord three times. We live out our call by picking up that cross and walking in the power of the Holy Spirit.

My book up to this point has been heavily focused on the importance of showing compassion toward and seeking justice for the marginalized populations among us. But as I've said in previous chapters, the Great Commandment (justice and compassion) must be done in tandem with the Great Commission, which includes reaching the lost and making disciples. We must never lose sight of the importance of disciplemaking, as that is at the core of the church's mission here on earth. Unfortunately, many churches (church leadership) have not prepared for the eventuality of reaching the new mission field—the New Samaria—because they never saw it coming. My fear is, If majority-culture church leaders are confused about how to do discipleship with people who are like them, how can they be expected to engage in discipleship with those who come from different backgrounds, cultures, traditions, and even languages? It can be an intimidating prospect. But this is the reality we are facing. The New Samaria is here to stay, and it's for our good because we must recalibrate our idea of who God's mission includes.

God delights in cultures and the diversity of his people all over the world, and even though we are all different, the meaning of discipleship has never changed. If we look to the New Testament, we can clearly see the way Jesus discipled his followers and glean important principles from his methods. I believe it is time for us to get back to the core of disciplemaking. So let's check our church programs, membership, and all cultural assumptions at the door. Let's strip it to the irreducible biblical core. The same truths will be true anywhere in the world, from Talcahuano, Madrid, and Rome to Beijing, Jerusalem, Nairobi, and Chicago, and even to the ends of the earth—Laredo, Texas. The core truth will fly in our neighborhood of Chinatown or Little Italy. These few simple principles will mean the same in the urban core and in suburban communities.

Let me make a distinction between being a disciple and being a leader. All of us are called to be disciples, while not all are called or gifted to be leaders. (By leader I mean elder, deacon, deaconess, or any ministry leader.) I've found that, in many churches, there is an overemphasis on finding leaders. We have so many ministries, groups, and programs that we need people to lead! This is often our way of getting members to transition from participating to serving (i.e., taking the practice of their faith to the next level). And don't get me wrong—Paul says, "Whoever aspires to be an overseer desires a noble task" (1 Timothy 3:1, NIV). However, I believe that our frequent talk about leaders discourages and distracts from the conversation about being a disciple. I think this is an important paradigm shift we all must make before we intentionally engage the New Samaria in our local churches. If we are creating an intentional culture of disciplemaking, then leaders will undoubtedly pop up. I will address the importance of equipping leaders in the next chapter.

Simple Mandate: Make Disciples

"Go therefore and make disciples of all the nations,
baptizing them in the name of the Father and of the
Son and of the Holy Spirit, teaching them to observe all
things that I have commanded you; and lo, I am with you
always, even to the end of the age." Amen.
MATTHEW 28:19-20

These are the final two verses in the Gospel of Matthew, and they are not the first time Jesus speaks about disciplemaking. They are a summation of what he has been saying from the very beginning. When he first called the disciples, he told them his intention was for them to "Come, follow me, . . . and I will send you out to fish for people" (Matthew 4:19, NIV).

Jesus had a simple process. There was little sideways energy. He didn't get drawn into Simon the Zealot's overthrow of the Roman occupation. The Pharisees couldn't draw him into a philosophical debate on whether they should pay taxes or not. When the people wanted to make him king, he was nowhere to be found. He did not seek to recruit the powerful people of his day. He did not brand his work or spend time working up a budget. He did not seek a building for training and teaching. Jesus' classroom was the highways, byways, boats, mountains, and people's homes. He was accessible to all, from the babies to the marginalized. He had a diverse group of followers and poured his life into them. I truly believe that sometimes we think we can do it better than Jesus, what with our access to beautiful buildings, lots of money, advanced technology, and believers in high positions of power. We have placed our trust in the wrong things.

In the remainder of this chapter, I want to focus on some of what I consider the irreducible core of disciplemaking. If we are serious about reaching the New Samaria and having an impact within the demographic shift we are experiencing, we need to get down to the basic core principles that will allow for reproduction and rapid mobilization.

Simple, Reproducible, Accessible, and Affordable

The disciplemaking model I learned as a student was simple. It did not include a library full of books. Our Bible studies included looking for observations, correlations, interpretations, and applications. We were specifically discouraged from using commentaries, as that was not relying on the Holy Spirit. We shared our efforts and sorted through all of our work, sifting for a community understanding. We internalized the message in 2 Peter 1:20, which says, "No prophecy of Scripture is of any private interpretation." We were taught to seek God's Word together. It was humbling and exciting. And it was easy to reproduce, no matter where I found myself in life.

When I went to seminary, I took Bible study methods my first semester. Guess what Professor Hendricks emphasized? Observation, interpretation, correlation, and application. No kidding, by the end of the first semester I was ready to quit seminary. My campus ministry had done such a fine job of discipling me that

I already knew the things seminary was teaching me! My professor was a prophet and convinced me to stay. The church structure that I had entered into told me that I needed that piece of paper to give me knowledge and credibility before entering into full-time ministry, so I went along and got not one but two seminary degrees.

This is not a diss on seminaries—I do believe there is a place for the training they give—but I believe we have placed too much emphasis on formal training and degrees in order to make disciples and to teach people how to make disciples. However, we should not confuse seminary degrees with disciplemaking.

If we truly want to prepare ourselves for the future of embracing Samerica, we need to make disciplemaking more accessible to everyone. In the book *Movements That Change the World*, Steve Addison asserts that "theological refinement resulted in the loss of vitality and movement decline."[2] I would not trade my seminary training, but I would rather have one hundred disciplemakers skilled in simple, reproducible, and accessible training than one hundred formally educated students. (My real preference would be to have seminarians who were also practically trained to be makers of disciplemakers. To have both would be a double blessing.)

Whatever model we use for disciplemaking should be affordable; no one should have to spend a lot of money to learn these methods. All we need is the Word of God, some basic tools, and a community of other saints, and we can do it. This is why the disciples turned the world upside down without extended training. They lived with the Word of God, lived in community, applied what they were learning, and then simply told other people what they were learning.

Separating Our Culture from God's Culture

I'm sure most of us have been involved in a ministry or a church that had their particular way of doing discipleship—a program, series, cycle, or booklet. Maybe it even had a catchy name and was branded with a beautiful design! While these tools can be helpful, the danger arises when our tools or methods become the only way, or they become the end rather than a way to the end.

In my years of full-time ministry, I've sorted through many, many programs with the goal of figuring out how to create a culture of disciplemaking in the church. This becomes extremely challenging in a multicultural setting because everyone is coming to the table with different ways of relating to God, traditions, and expectations about church. Christian leaders must be able to distinguish when their methods and programs are steeped in the majority culture. It is common for all of us as humans to start to think our way is the God-ordained way, especially when that's the only way we know. This is why when I do or teach discipleship, I don't like to stick to one program. Using different tools helps us develop perspective and make space for people who do it differently. We must have the cultural maturity to discern between what is an expression of our culture and what is the irreducible core of disciplemaking—and the only way to do that is to see how people from other cultures do it differently.

It is natural for people to let their culture twist the irreducible core of disciplemaking. Once when I was with a gathering of leaders, we divided up to pray and talk about how we made disciples in our different church contexts. They had the wise idea to put the ethnic minorities together in the same group. When we were alone, one of the leaders said, "Let's get something clear. I disciple my family, and that is it. We don't disciple like these white brothers in our church." I will not tell you his ethnicity because it could really have been a person of any race or culture. He had gotten to the point where his views on discipleship were clouded by his culture, not based on biblical principles. He had ventured far away from the irreducible core.

Dr. Tony Evans, a well-known African American pastor, speaker, and author, has spoken about the place of culture and how to approach our differences. He said: "Because we are so culturally sensitive, oftentimes culture will trump the Bible. And once you do that we're in a no-man's-land. . . .We've got to now bring our culture and our race under the authority of Jesus Christ, and that means under the authority of Scripture. [I have to] slam that home all the time. . . . Maybe you had some bad experiences, . . . [but] you can't dictate to the Kingdom."[3] I believe this quote applies to people from every culture, whether you're in the majority or the minority. Sometimes white Christians forget they have a culture too! As Daniel Hill points out in his article, "Witness or Whiteness?," not only is white culture real, but when it comes in contact with other cultures, it almost always wins. In the United States, and in the Western church, whiteness has become the "normal" by which we judge all other cultures.[4]

I know that begs the question about who decides what is the irreducible core of being a disciple and what is the cultural component. It can be argued that everything we do is steeped in culture—even Jesus' ministry was specific to the culture of his day. While this is certainly true, we must remember that the New Testament is full of cross-cultural ministry efforts, beginning with Jesus' ministry and on through the work of the apostles—and we can look to Jesus' example. We don't need a special divining rod to find the way through the maze of culture. The solutions are (1) trusting that the Jesus we see in the New Testament had that figured out, (2) putting Christ above culture, and (3) recognizing that man-made culture does not trump the culture of Christ. This requires cultural humility and a measure of adventure. Above all, we need to be willing to submit our way to his way.

When Jesus addressed the disciples' prejudice by speaking directly to the Samaritan woman at the well in John 4, we see

God's culture winning—inclusivity over separation. When God spoke to Peter in a vision about Cornelius in Acts 10, ordering him to violate the man-made conventions that a Jewish person should not enter the house of a Gentile, we see God's culture winning—hospitality over tradition. Jesus' ministry was never just among people like him. He set the example by living life among the Gentiles, the marginalized, and the poor.

We need cultural humility to see the culture of God. I will talk more about this in chapter 10, which is about unity. There are two important questions for us to be asking ourselves: Are we doing discipleship this way because it's the way we've always done it? Is there a better way? The only way to figure out the answers to these questions is to expose or immerse ourselves in other people's cultures, and we will begin to get a glimpse.

Life-on-Life Discipleship

A professor in seminary had a saying that "some things are better caught than taught." Most of us who are parents know that telling a child to go do something will not yield much success. But if you call them over to you and do something together, there is a much better likelihood they will learn. The disciples learned from Jesus because they followed him and watched him closely. There's a reason Jesus asked them to literally follow him—he knew that doing life together is the best curriculum.

I realize that not every church and ministry does discipleship this way, and this is one of the irreducible cores that we need to get back to. I have benefited from this type of discipleship, and it impacted me significantly. The first church I went to after I married and left The Navigators ministry was a Brethren church. The pastor, Wes Spradley, had lots of people clamoring for his time, and yet he made time for me. I was one of the few ethnic minorities in his church. He mentored me. He invited Julie and our kids to spend the night over at their house so we could talk late and rise early to visit. He let me go anywhere he went. I would drop in at his office when he was studying, and he would let me see how and what he was studying.

Wes may have thought I was a little strange, but I am forever grateful that he encouraged me to live life with him. He also learned a lot from being in relationship with me, as I was from a completely different background than him. Relationships are always two-way. We can learn a lot from diversity if we make time to invest in one another.

Humility and Authenticity

Our goal is to follow Jesus' model of multicultural disciplemaking; but let's be honest: He was perfect and we are not. Once while preaching on marriage at my church, I shared that Julie and I had recently had an argument. The next day a well-meaning brother stopped by to rebuke me. He said that the congregants needed to know that I had it all together! I told him I was sorry to disappoint him, but they might as well know it now—I am not perfect. But, also, I'm not satisfied. I invited him on a journey where we could stumble forward in life together.

Since we are not Jesus, we need to make sure we model humility and show that we are also works in process. Our ministry is an invitation to an honest, walk-in life and a call to mutual accountability. Here are a few ways to do this:

- Involve a diversity of people from different cultures in your discipleship team. Don't be afraid to fail or have cultural stumblings. Nothing ventured, nothing gained. Have the posture of a learner. Everyone loves a learner and enjoys teaching their point of view.

- Be quick to apologize if you make a mistake or have a mis-understanding. Humbling yourself does not lower yourself; it exalts the fact that God is at work in you.

- Help people find out what they are gifted in and then help them succeed in that. Engage in teamwork whenever possible and try your best to cultivate a sense of support and encouragement among your peers or your department. John Maxwell said, "Leaders become great, not because of their power, but because of their ability to empower others."[5]

- Invest in different people who represent the future of our church. Biblical truth is absolute, but its application over the generations has been fluid. Not everything will always be as it is today. Our approaches to issues of cultural engagement will continue to evolve and adapt. Our failure to engage and invest in demographics that represent the future has created a generational trust gap of our own making. We have stumbled forward as other generations of the church did, but now it is time to pass the church forward and let them sort through what will be of use to them in their future iteration of the church.

- If you are a man, this means intentionally making room for women. This is not just being a gentleman. It is seeking wisdom and talents from every quarter. Jesus' group of disciples was diverse in many ways: politically, educationally, financially, and in personality and gender. Women were involved in his ministry in significant ways, at times in ways that defied conventions of the day. If you look at the history of most church movements, you see women's enormous influence.[6] Be wise to include women of all cultures in significant ways, and they will have a significant impact on the growth and health of your church.

Create a Simple Disciplemaking Culture in Your Church

If you are on board with what you've read so far and are ready to create a culture of disciplemaking in your church, below I have outlined a few ways to start. If you are not yet reaching a diverse group of people, but you are ready to start, implementing these principles will ensure that you are prepared to engage them once they arrive—which will undoubtedly happen, I assure you!

1. Church leaders *must* be doing it. It all starts with the leadership of your church. If the pastor and church leaders aren't making disciples, make that a must in leader qualifications. Leaders must model passionate love for the Word of God, prayer, evangelism, and hospitality.

2. Communicate it. Have a simple, intentional process and common language for life-on-life disciplemaking. Make sure all leaders are able to communicate it. Talk about it from the pulpit. Repeat it often.

3. Celebrate it. Celebrate the discipleship relationships you are witnessing in your church. Instead of having random sermon illustrations, spotlight your people's success. Share stories in the bulletin. Be creative, and be sensitive to cultural proclivities of celebrating. Don't get stale. Some churches even have a banquet, retreat, or BBQ where they look back in celebrating and give goals for the future.

4. Be real and exercise grace. Encourage people to walk in obedience with Christ, but exercise grace. People don't like being guilted. Even subtle forms of encouragement to obedience are appreciated. I've heard of one church that subtly puts a rose in the vase on the piano whenever there is a conversion.

5. Allow other people to influence the disciplemaking process. Don't be married to the disciplemaking tools you have always used. Allow for different expressions of disciplemaking, and respect the fact that not all will be on the same track.

6. Do it in community. Make sure you have diverse hands executing the plan for disciplemaking. Have a diversity of genders, ethnicities, and ages involved (including the youth). Diversity adds creativity and expresses belonging. Bring the margins to the center. Don't expect them to pay their dues or get in line for leadership. If Jesus did that he would not have selected uneducated, uncultured, stinking fishermen.

7. Tie it all back. As much as possible, ask that every ministry be able to express how what they are doing encourages the disciplemaking process and outcome. All of the programs need to see themselves as parts of the whole, not as separate entities.

The most important thing is that our efforts be real, humble, and above all, solidly underpinned in the Word of God. It is so critical that people be allowed to put their hands on it and make it their own rather than it being handed down by the leaders.

Regarding Jesus' strategy for disciplemaking, Robert Coleman said, "This is one of the marvels of his strategy. It is so unassuming and silent that it is unnoticed by the hurried churchman. But when the realization of his controlling method finally dawns on the open mind of the disciple, he will be amazed at its simplicity and will wonder how he could have ever failed to see it before. Nevertheless, when his plan is reflected on, the basic philosophy is so different from that of the modern church that its implications are nothing less than revolutionary."[7]

He did not come with a strategy. He was not in a hurry. Most of us have heard the saying, "Culture eats strategy for breakfast every time"—meaning your strategic plan means nothing if the members have not bought into the culture. Let disciplemaking become part of your operating system, and you will set yourself up for future success. Always bring it back to the GC3. If you want to know if your irreducible principles are hitting the target, look for multiplication and transformation. In the book of Acts, the phrase "multiply," or a variation of it, is repeated six times. "Then those who gladly received his word were baptized; and that day about three thousand souls were added to them" (Acts 2:41). This is the test of the GC3. When you combine the Great Commandment to love your neighbors with the Great Commission to reach the lost and make disciples, you will undoubtedly see transformation.

REFLECTION

Consecrating Prayer: Lord, I accept the challenge to be your disciple and make disciples of all people. Help me to follow your example. Help me be faithful.

Head Work: Memorize Matthew 28:19-20: "'Go therefore and make disciples of all the nations, baptizing them in the name of the Father and of the Son and of the Holy Spirit, teaching them to observe all things that I have commanded you; and lo, I am with you always, even to the end of the age.' Amen."

Heart Work: Getting eternal life requires faith. But becoming Christlike requires faithfulness. Reflect on what Jesus said in Luke 9:23: "If anyone desires to come after Me, let him deny himself, and take up his cross daily, and follow Me."

Hands Work: Are you involved in a discipleship relationship? If you are not, try to find someone to disciple you. The goal is to become a committed follower of Christ, rather than a casual follower. Try to find a discipler who has a different ethnic or cultural background than you, and enter into the relationship with a learning and humble posture.

RESOURCES

- *Growing in Christ: A Thirteen-Week Course for New and Growing Christians* by The Navigators (available for purchase at https://www.navigators.org/resource /growing-in-christ/)
- "Navigator Disciplemaking Tool: Share God's Love with Your Neighbor" (free resource available at https://www.navigators.org/resource/neighbors)
- Book Suggestions: *Making Disciples Across Cultures* by Charles A. Davis; *DiscipleShift: Five Steps That Help Your Church to Make Disciples Who Make Disciples* by Jim Putman and Bobby Harrington; *The Deeply Formed Life* by Rich Villodas

CHAPTER 9

Equipping Leaders

*And He Himself gave some to be apostles, some prophets,
some evangelists, and some pastors and teachers, for the
equipping of the saints for the work of ministry, for the edifying
of the body of Christ, till we all come to the unity of the faith and
of the knowledge of the Son of God, to a perfect man, to the
measure of the stature of the fullness of Christ.*

EPHESIANS 4:11-15

AFTER I GRADUATED from Dallas Theological Seminary in 1987, my very first church plant was a multiethnic church in San Antonio, Texas. A majority of the church members were Hispanic, most of them recently out of the Catholic church, and they were hungry for a relationship with Jesus. I was eager to lead them along the road of discipleship, but I also wanted to raise up leaders. I found myself working around the clock to figure out how to do disciple-making and leadership training at the same time. The good thing is that if you have created a culture of discipleship in your church, people begin to discover their gifts and calling, and leaders begin to naturally emerge. But still, many of them felt unequipped to perform some of the leadership tasks I was asking them to do.

I tried many different approaches, and after about ten years my ultimate solution was to create a leadership training institute

EMBRACING THE NEW SAMARIA

in our church that required leaders to go through three years of training focused on theology, Bible study methods, disciple-making processes, and practical ministry, such as basic counseling. (Can you tell I was ambitious?) It was a big commitment, but many people followed through because they were hungry to learn. I didn't get to see the first cycle of training to completion, since I was called to leave the church and accept a job at my denomination's national office. But even before the first three years were over, several from the church were planning on continuing in full-time church ministry.

One thing I've learned in my decades of working for the Lord is that in order to reach immigrant and marginalized communities among us, training and equipping leaders is key. I define a leader as anybody who has an office or leads a group in a church. This includes a pastor, ministry leader, deacon, elder, or small group leader. Making disciples is important, as I made clear in chapter 8, but equipping leaders helps ensure that these disciples are moving forth with sound doctrine. Ultimately, by empowering leaders who are gifted in encouraging the makers of disciplemakers, we will be able to mobilize and multiply even quicker.

Research presented by Steve Addison in the book *Movements That Change the World* shows why the American Christian church is not experiencing rapid mobilization—it is because of our over-reliance on budget, building, and credentials. In a stinging rebuke Addison painfully points out that mainline churches were led by clergy who "preferred to *educate* their hearers rather than *convert* them."[1] Not much has changed. A case in point of the opposite: China is on course to become the world's most Christian nation by 2030, even though they have few buildings (many churches are underground), seminaries, and printing presses.[2] In fact, they are persecuted for congregating and reading the Scriptures. How do they do it? Not by waiting for an officiant! They read, they do, then they pass it on! They do not do fund drives. They do not quibble about the finer points of doctrine. They don't worry about the stains on their carpets.

In the United States, we place so much emphasis on formal theological training that we are unintentionally keeping the marginalized out of the center. Even though the requirements for leadership differ greatly between denominations, one thing is clear: The higher the educational requirement for ministry, the quicker that denomination is shrinking.[3]

A New Training Paradigm

As it is now, the gold standard for most church denominations is the Master of Divinity (MDiv), which requires a three-year course of study that prepares students to become ordained pastors in church settings, or leaders in parachurch ministries or other non-traditional Christian organizations. There are also various other Master of Arts degrees offered at seminaries that are increasing in popularity; they require a two-year course of study in subjects like ministry or leadership that can also be useful in a career of full-time ministry. However, if we want to succeed at reaching Samerica, we will need to adapt our leadership development techniques, which means veering away from how the church machine has always done things—and that means less formal theological training (seminary) and more nontraditional, nonformal, creative ways of equipping leaders with the tools they need to thrive. I can't even begin to tell you how many times credentialing and theological training have been obstacles to raising up immigrant and marginalized pastors and ministry leaders, but they don't have to be.

The next few things that I will write need to be understood in context. First, I thank God for the seminary training I received. All who have the opportunity to receive this kind of formal training should, but we who receive the training should not be an impediment to people God has gifted and chosen for their place in ministry. Secondly, we must work with what God is doing. If he gifts and calls someone to lead, who are we to stand in his way? We must recognize people who are gifted and called.

There are several problems with requiring a seminary education in order to serve in church ministry and leadership, especially as it relates to marginalized Christians, including people of color, immigrants, and women. Many marginalized leaders can handle and thrive in this academic world, but not all can, nor should they try. Here are some of the problems.

LANGUAGE BARRIERS

In the United States, immigrants from all over the world are living among us and attending our churches, many who are gifted leaders—yet English is not their first language, and this can be a barrier to achieving higher levels of education in this country. This is not to say they are not intelligent or highly capable—many are highly skilled or were educated in their home countries, but their education does not transfer over. Or some of them come from other countries that have experienced genuine Christian revival, and they are on fire for the Lord.

I remember, years ago, a regional leader from my denomination asked me to help him select a Latino assistant for his team. I recommended a man who I knew had fantastic leadership qualities, but my colleague expressed concern because his English was not very good, and deep down he doubted his capability. I pointed out to my colleague that our Latino brother was highly educated; in his home country, he was an attorney and an architectural engineer. I pointed out that while our Latino brother struggled a bit with English, he probably knew more English than my colleague knew Spanish. Unfortunately, he was not hired.

People of color in the United States are all too familiar with the discrimination and exclusion that occurs when someone's dominant language is other than English. Our church structures and seminaries cater to English speakers, making it difficult for immigrants to thrive in leadership positions and formal theological training programs.[4] If we are going to reach Samerica moving into the future, this absolutely needs to change.

COST BARRIERS

Seminaries, like graduate schools, can be cost prohibitive for some people who come from low-income backgrounds, as do many (though certainly not all) immigrants and people of color. If they are seeking to do full-time ministry in a low-income part of town, then it makes it even harder to pay back school loans.

Of course, this is not just a problem for marginalized communities; it is also becoming an obstacle for majority-culture leaders. In an article from Religion News Service, Cameron Trimble, CEO of the Center for Progressive Renewal, describes one of the reasons many students are leaving the Master of Divinity behind: "The crisis we have is that if you're graduating with a Master of Divinity you're likely graduating with some significant debt and then you'll struggle to find jobs and jobs that pay really low wages."[5]

This reality can affect anyone of any culture or race, but it disproportionately affects marginalized groups and people of color. We cannot expect everyone to be able to afford seminary, and we are missing out on many gifted pastors and leaders because of it.

CULTURAL CHALLENGES

Minority groups tend to disproportionately experience cultural challenges that lead to feelings of invisibility and loneliness, even if they were born here, speak English well, and are prepared for the academic rigor. It's an even bigger problem for women of color, given that these programs tend to be mostly male. In the book *Still Evangelical?*, Sandra Maria Van Opstal articulates the problem well as she describes the daily frustration she experienced while getting an MDiv at a highly reputable and well-known seminary:

> Despite the tens of thousands of pages I read while in seminary, I was never assigned a book by an ethnic minority scholar, let alone a Latinx theologian. My community's spirituality and perspectives were excluded as I learned about the history of Christianity. We skipped right from the early church to linger for months in the European white saviors of the reformation and then moved on to the white saviors of the great revivals. . . . I was never influenced by someone who came from my location. I never heard our voice in the classroom, and even worse, my classmates never heard the voice of my community.[6]

Being trained in an environment where your culture is in the minority and there are few in authority who understand your experience is mentally and emotionally exhausting. That's not to say we (marginalized leaders) shouldn't go, because we are needed in those spaces, and there are many who can benefit, endure, and excel at the training from seminary. But the reality is that we always have to do the contextualization ourselves because the training is not adapted to our communities.

The Question of Necessity and Relevance

The unfortunate reality is there is no guarantee that formal theological training will translate into credibility or even be much help in a marginalized church setting. As stated by John Dorhauer: "Getting a Master of Divinity is no longer assurance that, given how much is changing in the nature of the church, that those who graduate with an M.Div. are fully equipped to lead the churches that are emerging on the horizon."[7]

My experience has confirmed this reality. As a young man and a new believer, I played by everyone's rules to get formal training. After receiving my undergraduate degree, I attended one of the most prestigious independent seminaries in America to get trained on how to be a professional Christian. But even through all of that, I struggled to find my place after I graduated.

During my last year in seminary, the job board at DTS was filled with opportunities for most of my fellow graduates—but not for me. One of Professor Hendricks's sayings was, "If you preach the Word, they will beat the door down to hear you." I believed him. But the job board did not list any churches seeking a Hispanic pastor. There were many opportunities available in suburbia. There were even some opportunities at Asian American and African American churches, but it put a pit in my stomach that there were no Hispanic churches on that job board. Had I gone through all of that training just to end up going forever living outside of my skin? Little did I know that there were plenty of fish; I was just fishing in the wrong pond.

I hungered to see more churches with diversity, and after being in majority-culture settings for so long, I knew I had to serve around other Latino people. I knew most Hispanics were Catholic. I had seen some Baptist, Presbyterian, and Assemblies of God churches. But I wanted an opportunity to work in a low church, high disciplemaking culture. After much consideration and prayer, I decided to raise money and start a church.

I remember when I planted my first church, it took me several years to downshift from my academic mindset and reconnect with the people I was going to serve in under-resourced neighborhoods in San Antonio. I loved my church and had close relationships with the people. One member—a brother named David—told me to please quit using unnecessary big words in my teaching. Javier Galindo —a very educated brother and disciple of Christ— lovingly explained to me that he didn't want to know the truth, he wanted to feel the truth. He didn't need five plausible interpretations for every piece of Scripture. He simply wanted to know how to live his life in this world in a way that made him feel useful to God. It took me a while, but I had to learn how to become less cerebral in my teachings and meet my congregation where they were. Inside I am and always will be a *vato*[8] from the borderland. No one can ever force me to believe that someone needs "approved" and "credentialed" training—not even the biggest, most reputable Christian institutions—not as long as we have the Bible, the Holy Spirit, and a reconciled community that is committed to transformation.

If you are the leader of a church or Christian organization or institution and are ready to commit yourself to the equipping of immigrants, ethnic minorities, and other marginalized leaders, be encouraged! Your forward thinking will serve you well in the coming decades, as Samerica is our future. In order to be ready, you and your church or organization will need to develop a strategy on how to do this, and I will provide some concrete examples below. But first, there are a few things you should keep in mind.

The Importance of Trust and Mutuality

In chapter 1, "Recalibrating Our Vision," I wrote about John 4:35, where Jesus said to the disciples that there aren't four months until harvest like they thought. He instructed them to open their eyes and look at the fields, which are ripe for harvest. In this passage, Jesus was talking about two different harvests. The "four months then harvest" is the one you are already familiar with—you know when to plant, how to fertilize, and when to harvest. The second harvest he speaks of is the one we do not yet know. You may have even been poisoning it because you thought it was a weed, or you didn't care for its fruit. But now God has called you, as Jesus did the apostles, to reap this harvest that you did not work for. It will not be a simple task, but with humility and mutual trust we can go a long way.

Reaping this harvest will take learning on all sides. You can't treat it by default like the first harvest. It will require being a reconciled community, and to get there, we need to work through some trust issues. Especially in relationships between people of different backgrounds, ethnicities, races, and socioeconomic levels, trust needs to be established before working together. In the book *The Speed of Trust*, the author states:

> Trust impacts us 24/7, 365 days a year. It undergirds and affects the quality of every relationship, every communication, every work project, every business venture, every effort in which we are engaged. Contrary to what most people believe, trust is not some soft, illusive quality that you either have or you don't; rather, trust is a pragmatic, tangible, actionable asset that you can create—much faster than you think possible. I am also convinced in every situation nothing is as fast as the speed of trust.[9]

How do we develop trust? Much goes into this hard work, but if I had to distill it down to the essentials, I would say it boils down to (1) learning to listen well to one another, (2) being honest and open with one another, (3) sharing life with one another, and (4) finding common values. We cannot build up and equip people without first being "with" one another. When Jesus chose the disciples, he invited them to live life "with" him. If we try to train others before we connect with their realities in life, the whole process may be a failure. It is very much like a mentorship relationship, except in multiethnic contexts, you must expect some reverse mentoring, where the majority-culture person does much of the learning.

Many of us are used to mentoring being a one-way relationship, but Earl Creps in his book *Off-Road Disciplines* makes a great case for a special relationship in which the junior instructs the senior.[10] I think this is especially important in a cross-cultural setting. It's not enough to be willing to listen. A leader needs to have the courage to change gears and encourage the same in others.

Expect for intercultural/intergenerational reverse mentoring to take longer than the typical mentoring relationship. Because of history and people's experiences, it will take time to develop trust. One of the things I tell my family of the lighter hue is that they should let trust set the speed of ministry. It may be slower, but once trust is developed, going forward will be worth the effort and pay relational dividends.

The late Bill Hamel, former EFCA president, was my mentor even before we worked together. He took me under his wing, allowed me to share life with him, and did an excellent job of modeling reverse mentoring. It took several years of getting to know one another, but I recall the exact moment when I knew I truly trusted him. One time he took me to lunch at the World Market in Minneapolis, which was in the old Sears building. The basement had a food court filled with different kinds of ethnic and international foods, and we both chose the Mexican restaurant. I loaded up my plate and then had them hit me with the hottest hot sauce on top. Bill followed, and he also asked for the hottest. But the young lady refused to give him the good stuff! I asked her in Spanish why she wouldn't give him the hot sauce, and she replied in Spanish, "He is white and can't handle the hot stuff; I know he will make me take the food back." Immediately I responded, "Don't worry, he is one of us!" Finally, she agreed, and sure enough, Bill had no problem at all consuming the hottest hot sauce. I mused on that for a long time. Obviously being a reconciled community goes beyond developing a high tolerance for hot sauce—but I couldn't help but marvel at how quickly I vouched for him and declared, "He is one of us!" Our relationship had been through pain and gain, experienced through the many hours of talking about our hurt, our passion to see multiethnic multiplication, and our shared frustration at the one-size-fits-all training paradigm in the church. I knew that I could trust him, and I knew he would say the same about me.

Adaptive Training for Today's Off-Road Leaders

As I have already mentioned, not all churches and organizations allow for nonformal training as a ministerial credential—but as a New Samaritan mission field is coming into focus, some have been adapting the requirements, and some have even allowed equivalency to flourish. Recently, some seminaries have begun attempts to expand offerings to equip marginalized leaders by introducing nonformal theological training. For example, Dallas Theological Seminary offered an evening program called the Lay Institute that allowed lay Christians to take classes, enriching their understanding of theology and the Bible with no prior training or admission to DTS required. Denver Seminary has the IDEAL Institute, started by my friend Dr. Daniel Carroll, which is a lay-level ministerial program taught entirely in Spanish. Trinity Evangelical Divinity School has also been hosting GATEWAY nonformal theological training programs for years (more on GATEWAY below).

Below are a few examples of training structures that have gained some steam in recent years, allowing for alternatives to formal theological training. A fuller discussion of these examples would take a whole book in itself. My desire in providing these examples is to encourage my fellow Christian leaders to think outside the box, to break the mold, and to pray for creativity from the Lord to adapt to your particular context. See how God is working among you, and join him in the process.

CHURCH-BASED LEADERSHIP TRAINING

I shared at the beginning of this chapter that after many years and much trial and error, I eventually created a three-year leadership training for my first church plant, which included theology, Bible study methods, leadership principles, and practical skills training, like counseling and mentoring. This is something that any church could implement with a little planning as a way to equip ministry leaders in their context. We required people to engage in discipleship before entering into this leadership program. In terms of logistics, there was a prescribed yearly schedule, and we found facilitators to teach in their areas of ability. Opportunities for participants to practice what they were learning were incorporated into the program. At the end of the three years, there would be a certificate ceremony.

CLUSTER-BASED THEOLOGICAL TRAINING

In this model, a variation of church-based leadership training, the curriculum is based on a denominational doctrinal statement, allowing leaders from local churches to participate together. I guided an EFCA team that started a model like this called EFCA GATEWAY,[11] and the recipients I had in mind were immigrant and ethnic minority leaders. It is an affordable and accessible twelve-module training program that teaches both theology and practical skills for ministry in a local context. Each training is contextualized by language, allowing people who are not native

English speakers to participate and thrive. After completion of the program, graduates receive a Gateway certificate and can apply to enter into the credentialing process for the denomination. In addition to being affordable (the whole class costs $300) and accessible, it is also transferable. Some people have returned to their home countries and been able to use the training abroad.

BOOT CAMPS

This kind of model is less about broad theological training and more about equipping leaders with startup skills that will allow them to execute specific church-multiplication endeavors, such as church planting. This model typically requires about twenty hours, either over a weekend or during the week. In the EFCA's church-planting boot camp,[12] we offer the class in both English and Spanish, equipping Latino leaders with the knowledge and skills to plant healthy churches in their communities. Each participant is assigned a coach, and the facilitators of the class are church planters who have been successful at reaching marginalized populations. It is affordable, accessible, and transferable.

• • •

Even though I used EFCA examples for all of these methods, I've found very similar efforts in other denominations and organizations. (I will refrain from trying to list them all, because I'm sure I would miss some and disappoint good friends.) But the important takeaway here is that these off-road trainings are not just limited to denominations. Independent churches and parachurch organizations are also using methods such as these, which is a big change in the right direction. Moving into church-based and denomination-based training has accelerated the planting of churches and the revitalization of disciplemaking. The denomination I serve has doubled the number of ethnic minority and immigrant churches as a result of focusing attention on justice, compassion, disciplemaking, and nonformal training over the last fifteen years. While there is reason to be pleased about this, we must not be satisfied. The next fifteen years will be the real test of effectiveness.

Will we be a church that can succeed at training leaders of color, immigrants, and the marginalized, and that invites them to join us in the mission of God among us? I am confident we can, but we must think outside the box. Not all will be full-time leaders; some will be bivocational tentmakers.[13] In fact, there are many that consider bivocational ministers more effective because they are more connected to their congregations. David Spenser, an African American pastor who graduated from Dallas Seminary but is also a professional musician, once told me that even if his church were able to pay him, he would still choose bivocational ministry because of the connections to the community it affords him. This is consistent with how many church members in the early church viewed their leaders. According to Rodney Stark, "Religious leaders have greater credibility when they receive low levels of material reward in return for their religious service."[14] I am not advocating to not compensate ministers of the church, but just trying to keep the matter in perspective.

As our countries move into a post-Christian era, many ministries will have to start becoming self-supporting, and I believe the main way we will do this is by bivocational ministry. But marginalized and ethnic minority leaders have already been in that season for a long time. Just as Jesus equipped the woman at the well to testify about Jesus to the Samaritans, so must we find people who will lead the way and spread the gospel in their families, communities, and networks. Our opportunity is now. The New Samaria will depend on it.

REFLECTION

Consecrating Prayer: Lord, help us become a church that identifies and equips leaders from diverse ethnicities, cultures, genders, and socioeconomic levels. Help us think creatively about training. Remove our blinders that keep us bound to the ways we've been taught.

Head Work: Think about the Christian leaders in your life who have influenced your spiritual journey. Did their backgrounds reflect the diversity of God's Kingdom? How did they shape your views on what it takes to become or be a leader in the church?

Heart Work: Reflect on whether your views on leadership have allowed room for marginalized people who are gifted and called. What is God calling you to change about your posture toward new models of equipping leaders?

Hands Work: Assess your bookshelf and count how many of your books are authored by people of color. How many are authored by women? Commit yourself to being led and taught by marginalized leaders by buying and reading more of their books. Start now!

RESOURCES

- CCDA (Christian Community Development Association) Institute Online provides courses on developing urban leaders, empowerment, reconciliation, etc., to help you create holistic transformation in your community. Gain access to the courses for minimal cost at ccda.org /courses-overview.
- Book Suggestions: *Churches, Cultures & Leadership* by Mark Branson and Juan Martinez; *The Hammer & The*

Pulpit by Barry Hannant. More and more leaders are having to learn to be bivocational pastors. This book is critical for equipping immigrant and ethnic minority leaders for the future.

be the new Samaria

CHAPTER 10

One Reconciled Community

*Therefore if there is any consolation in Christ, if any comfort
of love, if any fellowship of the Spirit, if any affection and mercy,
fulfill my joy by being like-minded, having the same love, being
of one accord, of one mind. Let nothing be done through selfish
ambition or conceit, but in lowliness of mind let each esteem
others better than himself. Let each of you look out not only
for his own interests, but also for the interests of others.*

PHILIPPIANS 2:1-4

A FEW YEARS AGO, there was a church in Texas that was expand-
ing their vision of God's Kingdom by becoming an intentional
multiethnic community. They had done the hard work of getting
to know their neighbors, growing in love, and reaching out with
the hope of making disciples among them. They decided to start a
Spanish-language service, so they hired a part-time Latino pastor
to lead the services. Once everything was in place to begin, the
leadership team from the English-speaking congregation realized
there was one point of theology in which the Spanish-speaking
leaders disagreed—and they wanted to come to an agreement on
this point before moving forward. The English-speaking leadership team had been extremely generous and encouraging the entire
time, and their request was not necessarily unrealistic, but the

last-minute change made the Spanish-speaking leaders uncomfortable. They did not feel called to change their position on this theological point. Both sides were to the point of grieving. After much prayer and consideration, the English-speaking leaders agreed to not make it a point of separation. In fact, the leadership team made it clear that, even though the theological nuance was still important to them, they valued the relationship more.

To be honest, it is rare that I see an example like this of humility and deference to the minority. The impact of this decision was tremendous. It generated lots of love and mutual trust, and the result was a further melding of hearts. At the business meeting where it took place, the white church took on the Hispanic pastor as full-time staff and elected members of the Hispanic church as elders. Eventually, the Hispanic pastor became the outreach pastor for the whole ministry. Unfortunately, stories of unity such as these are rare, but if we are going to embrace the New Samaria of the future, we must learn how to be reconciled as one community.

While there is much to admire about being obedient to God in seeing, loving, and reaching the New Samaria, we must also succeed at *being* the New Samaria. What do I mean? In this fourth part of the book, which I consider the most profound, especially in light of the accelerating demographic shift, we will focus on how to be one body, one community of believers, that not only transforms lives but transforms the community around us. As I've reiterated throughout the book, the true test is whether the Great Commandment and the Great Commission are leading to the Great Transformed Community (GC3). In order to get to the point of true transformation, we must be one reconciled community.

Why Is Unity So Hard?

The word *unity* is thrown around a lot by Christians, especially optimistic ones, as a way of describing the vision for God's people here on earth. Anyone who has a foundation of Christianity understands that division among God's people is bad, and unity among his believers is what we should strive for. Sounds good . . . on paper. But in reality, not very many people have a true understanding of what it means, what it looks like, or even if it's possible. Can we really expect people of all ethnicities, races, socioeconomic levels, and political views to come together as one? It's almost impossible to get a grasp on unity, especially when we log in to social media every day and our division and hate is staring us in the face.

As I write this chapter, the United States has been in the midst of racial and political unrest for some time. We have been seeing a disproportionate number of black people being killed by police, racial unrest, disagreements over the role of law enforcement, riots in our cities, neighborhood disparities, housing inequality, unfair treatment of immigrants and refugees, family separation at the border, and I could go on and on. This is a description, not a prescription of indictment. Politicians on both sides promise solutions that somehow evaporate after they are elected. The global pandemic has disproportionately affected people of color because our structures have set them up with the least ability to fight it off.

To be honest, I think more believers are paying attention to the political squabble than are listening to God. It's all too common to see Christians pointing fingers about the immorality of one political party, when it is reported that the other party has similar issues. We are looking for "salvation by government."[1] Don't get me wrong. There are truly substantive issues at stake, and the role of government is important, but in this cultural moment it seems that we are no longer capable of listening to one another. We are called as Christians to use our prophetic voices to call out what is wrong and to influence change in this world, but it's hard to be taken seriously when we can't seem to agree with one another. This is not what Jesus intended for us.

It's not hard to see what is stopping us from achieving unity of spirit. The injustice we see around us will never come to a complete end—at least not until Jesus returns and establishes his Kingdom here on earth. But in the meantime, two of our biggest impediments are a sense of entitlement/superiority among majority-culture folks and suspicion and lack of trust among people of color.[2] We will never move beyond our conflicting values and theological differences unless we can humble ourselves and try to see from a perspective different from our own.

Our differences do not surprise God. He knew that our sinful nature would make it difficult for us to love across our differences. Yet, God clearly calls us to a standard of unity that will glorify him. In Ephesians 4:1-6, Paul writes:

> I, therefore, the prisoner of the Lord, beseech you to walk worthy of the calling with which you were called, with all lowliness and gentleness, with longsuffering, bearing with one another in love, endeavoring to keep the unity of the Spirit in the bond of peace. There is one body and one Spirit, just as you were called in one hope of your calling; one Lord, one faith, one baptism; one God and Father of all, who is above all, and through all, and in you all.

How the Church Got to This Point

Most of us can't see the unity spoken of in Ephesians 4 in our country or world right now. Yes, there are glimpses of it every now and then, and praise God for those glimpses! But what we tend to see every day is arguing on social media, a lack of civility in our discussions about issues, and finger pointing and blaming. Meanwhile, when we go to church on Sundays, it is still the most racially segregated hour of the week. There are many factors that have led to this point, and while I can't address all of them in this book, I want to address how our history of missions and church-planting principles contributed to our current reality.

In the 1980s, our country experienced a "church growth movement" that turned oneness and unity on its head. Christian denominational leaders and church planters turned a missions principle called the homogeneous unit principle (or HUP) into a strategy that inadvertently ignored the poor and the marginalized here in America. (I briefly discussed this in chapter 2, when I gave the example of Saddleback Sam, the fictional target of Rick Warren's church.) In the 1970s, a missiologist and founding dean of the School of World Mission at Fuller Theological Seminary applied the homogeneous unit principle, the idea that (1) church growth would be more effective if churches focused more on the proclamation of the gospel and less on social concerns, and (2) churches would overcome growth barriers if they focused on a specific ethnolinguistic community. Many church leaders agreed, and this became the dominant strategy for church growth over the last few decades. In *The Next Evangelicalism*, Soong-Chan Rah details the history of this church growth movement in the United States, stating that the principles "prioritized an individualized, personal evangelism and salvation over the understanding of the power of the gospel to transform neighborhoods and communities." Furthermore, the HUP has "resulted in an American evangelicalism incapable of dealing with the reality of a growing cultural pluralism and ethnic heterogeneity."[3]

Adopting this kind of strategy legitimized the very thing Jesus spoke against in John 4, when the disciples balked at him for speaking to a Samaritan woman. The American church officially turned our eyes away from our very own Samerican mission field. It provided a church growth strategy that unintentionally lowered the missional bar to reach out to our neighbors who are different than ourselves. It became a mirror-mirror-on-the-wall branding effort to focus on people we could easily reach because they looked like us. Mission experts were relatively quick to point out that there was no biblical support for the HUP, but the excitement for the American Tower of Babel was already too seductive. And the tipping-point clock kept on ticking.

Lo and behold, churches really did grow. This strategy fed the megachurch mentality—the bigger the better! Research showed that, "American megachurches use stagecraft, sensory pageantry, charismatic leadership and an upbeat, unchallenging vision of Christianity to provide their congregants with a powerful emotional religious experience."[4] A study that evaluates churches' biblical effectiveness[5] demonstrated that some of these big churches did indeed get people started with Christ, and for that we must celebrate; people coming to Jesus is always a good thing. But they are not effective at moving them on to disciplemaking maturity. Some of these churches in the study were good at accepting the criticism and making adjustments, but many others who copied their form were satisfied with the size and notoriety. Conferences were held everywhere on how to become a megachurch. And I don't just want to pick on megachurches. Smaller churches were quick to criticize, but many of those were not reaching the poor and the marginalized either. In fact, the debate itself about megachurches and TV evangelists became a huge missional distraction. In general, Christians grew comfortable with being entertained. The bar was lowered, and the seeds of missional hurt were sown in our "success." Christian maturity and sacrificial commitments to real racial unity and diversity were dismissed. Many of these churches did not reflect the diversity of America. The church was filled with thousands of people all watching a few people do ministry, while there were still thousands in great need of equipping to do the real work of the church. And the tipping-point clock kept on ticking.

Lest we forget—there have always existed large ethnic minority and immigrant churches. In fact, the immigrant church has experienced some of the most dynamic church growth in the United States, oftentimes without much financial and denominational support. They have served a unique role in meeting the linguistic, spiritual, and social needs of immigrant communities, and there is much we can learn from them. This reality is unknown to a lot of majority-culture Christians who have been insulated in white, mainstream evangelicalism. Even though majority-culture churches have not done a great job of reaching out to immigrants, Jesus has been present there and working for as long as these communities have been around. But, just as the ignoring of immigrant communities has led to much inequality, so has the marginalization of these ethnic minority churches. Few sought out the hard work of oneness and unity, because the structures we set up for ourselves gave us an excuse to continue ignoring one another.

In the last decade, the homogeneous unit principle has been looked upon less favorably and even criticized by missiologists and church planters. René Padilla, an Ecuadorian evangelical theologian who has been vocal in his criticism of the HUP, put it well:

It may be true that "men like to become Christians without crossing racial, linguistic or class barriers" but that is irrelevant. Membership in the body of Christ is not a question of likes or dislikes, but a question of incorporation into the new humanity under the Lordship of Christ. Whether a person likes it or not, the same act that reconciles one to God simultaneously introduces the person into a community where people find their identity in Jesus Christ rather than in their race, culture, social class, or sex, and are consequently reconciled to one another.[6]

As older generations have begun to retire and younger generations take over, we've seen an increase in the desire for an alternative approach in which diversity in church settings is seen as an advantage. Multiethnic churches are emerging at a rate we've never seen before. In 1998, 6 percent of churches of all faiths in the US were multiracial; in 2019, that number rose to 16 percent. Mainline Protestant multiracial churches rose from 1 percent to 11 percent, and evangelical Christian multiracial churches rose from 7 percent to 23 percent.[7] While this progress is good, we have a long way to go toward achieving oneness and unity. I will write more about multiethnic churches in chapter 11.

What Does Unity Look Like?

For some people, unity is extremely hard to grasp because we think we will have to concede our convictions, culture, or values in order to make space for opposing views, cultures, and beliefs. What we so easily forget is that in Christ we all have the same common foundation. Achieving unity does not mean that one people group wins and another people group loses. Unity is no reference to subordination of race, nationality, gender, or anyone's worldview. Unity and oneness in Ephesians is in reference to very basic core doctrines and the person of God. There is no unity of democracy, or politics, or entitled group, or marginalized group. We are called to align to God, not to a human identity. "One" does not mean someone disappears. "One" is not your way or the other way. We are not talking about winners or losers. "One" here is God's way. We are called to align to God's mission. We are called to align to God's body.

In the book *Disunity in Christ*, social psychologist Christena Cleveland describes various research studies that show how focusing on our common identity helps break down barriers in cross-cultural situations, ultimately helping us achieve unity. The first step is to start thinking of ourselves as one large in-group (follow-ers of Jesus), as opposed to *us* versus *them*. She explains that when *they* (people who are different than us) become *we*, then

- we naturally like them a whole lot more;
- we're more open to receiving helpful criticism from them;
- we forgive them more easily and are less likely to expect them to experience collective guilt; and
- we treat each other better.[8]

That is our one hope for unity. If we seek to be a reconciled community in the New Samaria—consisting of many different cultures, ethnicities, and languages—we must focus on our common identity in Christ. That means that while there are consistent microcultural adaptations, political modulations (even political parties have swapped sides on issues), and risings and fallings of nations, God does not change. Here is the interesting thing we need to grasp: God authored the sending out from the Garden of Eden. He scattered the peoples from Babel. He scattered the church from Jerusalem. Only God can put us together again. But it will not happen by all of us being the same. He does not call us to forget who he made us in our diversity. He calls us to use our diversity, our privilege, our identity, our brokenness, to form what I like to think of as a mosaic. A mosaic by definition is a combination of diverse elements that form a coherent picture or pattern. I believe this is actually coming into focus, but we need to open our eyes and come together to see it.

Cranberry Relish with Jalapeño

My wife (Julie) and I are about as different as two people can be. She is a farm girl; I am a city boy. She is from the Fargo, North Dakota, area. I am from the borderland of Laredo, Texas. She is of the whitest tribe—Norwegians. I am a Latino/indigenous mestizo. When we met, she was Protestant; I was Catholic. She was a go-to-church-every-Sunday kind of saint. I wasn't. She was (is!) gorgeous; I was a half-tamed lowrider. After being married for a while, we took a computer evaluation as a couple of our compatibility on sixteen points of personality. The report came back with three asterisks at the bottom explaining that it had never evaluated a couple so different.

Our marriage at the beginning was painful and confusing. Before we got married, we would visit friends every night. After we got married, she said we couldn't be visiting friends every night anymore. I was scared and felt trapped. She also announced that we would be going to church every Sunday. I thought, *We go to Bible studies two or three times a week. Doesn't that count?* Nope. The union was challenging because we (well, I more than she) had lots of maturity issues to work out. There were many tears and laughs. My tears, her laughs (just kidding about the laughs). Julie also began to loosen her grip on cultural habits in order to accommodate me. Before marriage she was not much of a people person. She is an introvert by nature, and her Norwegian family were not much for hugging or showing physical affection. Imagine her reaction when I was called to be a pastor of a church. After much prayer, she also heard from God that this was the right call for our family. When we purchased our new home, the carpet in the living room wore out after three months because of all the people from church coming over to our home. She even became a hugger!

But despite our drastic differences, our union was fruitful. She saw things I didn't see and vice versa. We complemented each other in planting churches in ways that I can't even articulate here. We discipled people in ways I never considered. The nail on the wall that everything hung from was our love for Jesus and shared mission to make disciples among all people. We helped each other to see beyond our individual perspectives. While she was not a people person, she knew how to invest in people in ways I didn't. I walked into the room with my mouth flapping. She slipped into the church serving people and making them feel like family. As long as we kept our eyes focused on our common identity in Jesus, we were able to loosen the grip on our smaller cultural identities that we had held onto for so long.

Julie is an arch traditionalist, so Christmas is always done the same way, with the same foods. All of the women in her family were taught to make cranberry relish in a very specific way—cranberry and orange peels ground in an old-fashioned crank grinder. I love that she delighted in making this every year, but in all honesty, it was a little bland for my taste. One Christmas, she placed a second dish of relish on the table specifically for me. Everyone looked at me as I cautiously took a bite. To my surprise, it was awesome! Julie had used all the same ingredients with one magical addition—ground up jalapeños. This simple act made me feel validated and loved. I tell this story as a way of illustrating how it is possible to bring together people with individual cultural identities and somehow form a new common identity. This does not mean that we must completely leave behind our individual cultures. Doing so would mean erasing or ignoring a beautiful part of who we are! It didn't happen immediately, but after a few years of living life together we began to discover ways to practice our individual traditions with a twist—like cranberry relish with jalapeño![9]—and that twist is sometimes the key to breaking down divisions and being reconciled to one another.

I know this is not a book on cross-cultural marriage, but I do believe marriage gives an excellent illustration of the unity that we must seek with one another as believers. After four decades of being married to my Nordic wife, as well as several decades of cross-cultural ministry, I've learned many things, but let me share with you these three:

1. Unity across cultures is "good trouble" intended by God. Relationships with people different than you, whether through language, age, nationality, or socioeconomic level, will challenge your perspectives on life and faith. The people who challenge you are made in the image of God! This world is not meant for our ease and rest—that will come—but here and now, God is watching us as we try to bring order out of a disorderly world. Loving others and being united in mission is not easy, but it is worth it.

2. You never "arrive," even after a lifetime of work. This is not something that can be done quickly. Some people, churches, or organizations say they want diversity, so they launch a diversity initiative in order to train their members and recruit ethnic minorities. Unfortunately, many think that once the diversity initiative is over, they are done, and they move on to the next initiative. That is not how this works. Like marriage, it is a lifelong process. We may take one step forward and then two steps back, but one thing is for sure—it keeps us turning to God. Cross-cultural unity is the gift that keeps on giving.

3. Being in relationship with people different than us keeps life interesting! Over the years, I've encountered many Christians who are so comfortable in their Christian walk that they can't fathom spiritual challenges. When they are faced with something hard, they choose to ignore it. It's like we've been lulled into a spiritual sleepwalk in which we simply go through the motions without much thinking. When we are in relationship with Christians who are

different than us, whether theologically or culturally, we get a whole new perspective on God. Our walk will never get dull. There may be difficult moments, but God promises us an adventure.

Whenever I hear the news about the division in our country, it's painfully obvious that the world doesn't have it together. I think most of us can agree on that. What an incredible testimony it would be if the church could be a model for unity and love! There will always be a place for homogeneous, monolingual settings that meet the linguistic, spiritual, and social needs of non-English-speaking immigrants. However, the needs of their second- and third-generation, American-born children are entirely different. We are witnessing a new culture and identity emerge among younger generations where multiculturalism is the norm. We need to let go of old church paradigms that focus on a specific ethnolinguistic community and move toward a multiethnic, multicultural vision. This means that a culture of whiteness that has long been centered in Western evangelicalism must be set aside for a culture of Christian unity. People of all ethnicities and socioeconomic levels should be able to come together and feel welcome. Theological differences should be explored. The Great Commandment and the Great Commission should be pursued equally, without one taking priority over the other. This is what biblical unity looks like, and this is what the New Samaria will require of us.

I am an eternal optimist. I refuse to declare that our dance has turned to death or some other fatalistic epitaph. I see this cultural moment as an opportunity for our church to walk the walk. We should reemphasize the elements that helped the early church stand out from a morally bankrupted society. Rodney Stark cites several areas where the church separated itself from the culture of selfishness centuries after the death of Christ. The church excelled in the midst of crisis and plagues as an entity of "social service and community solidarity."[10] They were extremely accommodating to multicultural communities.

The darker it is, the brighter the bride of Christ can shine if we live out Jesus in unity. Instead of giving birth to death, let's give birth to a season of unity that transforms our siloed churches into staging grounds for reconcilers to be the hands, feet, and heart of the Lord. Pass that baton into the hands of the New Samaritans, those who have been marginalized for most of their lives, and the church will live.

REFLECTION

Consecrating Prayer: Lord, send your outpouring of unity. Without you I doubt it is possible. Maybe this demographic shift will bring a sense of urgency. Still, Lord, give us a hope that the heavenly vision can be lived here on earth. Let your Spirit fall on us again with fresh fire.

Head Work: Tune your ears this week to the many devices of the evil one to divide the people of God. Keep a pocket notebook or sheet of paper to note these many devices. In each case, think of one way followers of Jesus could counter this divisive device.

Heart Work: Reflect on which type of people it is hardest for you to come together with in unity. Why do you think that is?

Hands Work: Take an opportunity this week to speak out for unity. Don't brutally condemn but call out the works of divisiveness. Notice how divisiveness easily melts when you give voice to it. Then consider standing up for someone being spoken of cruelly.

Open your mouth for the speechless,
In the cause of all who are appointed to die.
Open your mouth, judge righteously,
And plead the cause of the poor and needy.
PROVERBS 31:8-9

RESOURCES

- Study passages in the Bible about the body of Christ and its differences, specifically 1 Corinthians 12 and Ephesians 4.
- Book Suggestions: *Be the Bridge* by Latasha Morrison; *The Beautiful Community* by Irwyn L. Ince Jr.; *One: Unity in a Divided World* by Deidra Riggs

CHAPTER 11

Multiethnic Ministry and Transforming Communities

*I dare to dream and hope of the great diversity
of the various nationalities of the world, but no longer
divided into enemies, free enough of racial and cultural
prejudices of the past to be able to love one another
as each is, free enough to learn from one another,
free enough to value and respect one another.*

FATHER VIRGILIO ELIZONDO,
THE FUTURE IS MESTIZO:
LIFE WHERE CULTURES MEET

I MENTIONED IN CHAPTER 10 that the US has seen an increase in multiethnic churches in the last couple of decades. Many denominations and church networks are recognizing the need to diversify their congregations. This is a step in the right direction, as it indicates that more Christians are recognizing the need to change the way they do church and being open to learning from different kinds of people. And it certainly is a step toward achieving unity in the Christian body. In truth, however, the heart of the matter is that churches need to be obedient in reaching their neighborhoods, repenting from the sins of injustice, and fighting for the vulnerable—whether they are of the same ethnicity/culture or not. This is not just about race and ethnicity. If you live in a homogeneous neighborhood with little ethnic diversity, there is no need to feel guilty. A multicultural ministry doesn't just mean many ethnicities. It could mean being open to welcoming different generations or marginalized populations, such as those experiencing poverty, homelessness, or disability. Basically, look around your church and ask yourself, *Who is not represented? Who are we missing?* Whatever your answer, start there.

This chapter will lean into the elements of multicultural ministry and transformative communities, because I do believe this is where we are headed for the future. It is not meant to be exhaustive or even delve into the nuances of logistical implications. There are other good books that will get into the details of those matters. I aim to give an overview of several different multicultural/justice-oriented models and provide some correctives that people tend to ignore.

Multiethnic Ministry Models

If you are ready to make the pivot to multiethnic ministry, I offer a few different models below. I understand that all churches are at different starting points, so some places may not fit neatly into a particular model, but I provide these simply to help you start thinking about what your next step might be.

1. *Intentional transition from monocultural to multicultural.* The first model describes churches that were originally monocultural but intentionally transition into a multicultural and justice-oriented church in response to demographic changes in their communities. They change their vision and mission statements, make their services more welcoming to other cultures, and become more focused on compassion and justice efforts in their community. I truly believe this is a high and holy calling because of how painful it can be in the process. However, if they engage in

adaptive leadership and let themselves be comfortable in the discomfort for a while, the benefits are truly worth it.

You can expect some of your congregation to leave in disagreement with the changing mission. That's okay. You can expect many growing pains as you develop a new identity. That's okay too. If you are part of a church that might be leaning in this direction, I encourage you to equip yourself with mentors and guides who can help you through this messy but rewarding terrain.

2. *Multicultural and justice-oriented via a second-language service.* This model makes a lot of sense for multilingual churches who want to start reaching immigrants in their neighborhoods. (I would venture to say that this model has accounted for 25 to 35 percent of church growth in many denominations.) When your neighbors speak a different language, sometimes the best approach is to start a new service in that language. Let me make it clear: This approach is different than simply renting space in your building to a completely different church. It is only a multicultural ministry if the two congregations consider themselves to be the same church, and they share mission statements, doctrine, leadership, or a budget. You should see a lot of sweet relationships and sharing happening in this model, and the close proximity becomes a great blessing as people share food, vision, labor, and differing anointings of God. If the two services happen at the same time, a family could attend together, and the members of the family could choose which language suits them best (language preference varies by generation). It opens vistas that each service could not see before they joined. I've seen situations where the neighborhood changes so much that the majority and

minority composition of the church flops. This is why it is so important to have a solid shared mission and mutual respect and trust.

Some churches attempt to keep the congregations together and use translation equipment for the second language. This might be a temporary bridge, but it's not ideal because a translated sermon typically lacks the nuance necessary for the listeners to get the most out of it. In a situation like this, the church must offer a great deal more to the second-language congregants, like cultural- and language-specific ministries that meet their practical needs, in order to bridge the gap.

3. *Two monocultural churches merge into a multicultural and justice-oriented ministry.* Usually this model involves two churches who encompass different cultures but speak the same language (like a black and white church), but it certainly could also apply to churches who speak different languages. This model makes the most sense when there are two churches in the same community with similar visions, but one or both are limited in resources. Since they complement each other, they decide to join together. I've seen this model work best when both churches close and then relaunch as a new church after the mission, values, strategies, and leadership details have been recast. This approach can be very challenging and requires lots of coffee, communication, mutual trust, and a solid understanding of details.

I foresee this transitioning/merging model happening a lot in the future as we reach the demographic tipping point. The key here is that both churches must enter into it with a humble attitude and approach the transition with open hands and a willingness to learn. I strongly suggest finding a mentor who can walk alongside the leadership through this process. If they are successful, it can become one of the most Kingdom-minded experiences one can behold.

4. *Intentional multiethnic and justice-oriented church planting.* If denominations and networks are in tune to the demographic changes of our country and doing their vision casting accordingly, then they should already be strategizing this model. An intentional plan is necessary because if it is not stated from the get-go, people will default back to "the ways we used to do it" as soon as things get complicated and hard. It's hard to flesh out this model in detail because regional context plays a big role in what it looks like practically speaking, but the most important step here is training up future church planters in the values of multiethnicity and justice.

I can't begin to tell you just how frustrated I've felt in situations when I'm in a meeting with fellow denominational leaders/church planters and I interject a reminder that we need to be aiming to reach "all people," and they immediately respond with a comment like, "Well of course, that's a given." My response to them is, "No, it's not." If we don't intentionally plan for multiethnic, multilingual, and multicultural churches, then it won't just happen— especially if everyone in leadership is from the majority culture. We must be intentional, include this value in our vision and mission, and do the hard work of training future leaders if we want to reach the New Samaria in the coming decades.

5. *Christian community development (CCD) focus.* A more justice-oriented model that sometimes overlaps with the models listed above is one that places an intentional focus

on community development. A church could start with this vision in mind, or it could pivot into a CCD model when it is ready. Either way, this kind of church (no matter what the ethnic makeup) will use its building not just for the needs of the church but also for the needs of the neighborhood. All churches and communities are different, but a good place to start is by looking to see what the greatest needs of your community are. Sometimes it involves efforts in housing and economic development, affordable medical services, or educational programs. In this model, the church is more than just a place for spiritual needs; it will become a place that takes a holistic approach to caring for the community.

6. *Business incubators.* This model is an interesting twist on Christian community development, as it includes the additional layer of churches becoming small business incubators. In low-income communities, this model seeks to provide people a path out of poverty (it is the "give a fish" versus "teach to fish" proverb in action). There is typically a small team of people, consisting of business experts or church staff with extra time, who help neighbors or church members start small businesses, with a small percentage going toward church offerings, which lessens the church's reliance on tithes. Mark DeYmaz talks about this model in his book *The Coming Revolution in Church Economics* in the context of the church's need to reevaluate our approach to finance and funding moving into the future.[1] As we continue adapting to the New Samaria, not only will more ministers become bivocational, but more churches should consider taking on this kind of model in order to help empower their communities.

7. *Organically multicultural.* I must say, this organic model is much rarer than the others. Most of the time it takes real intentionality to become a multicultural and justice-oriented community, but every now and then we see examples of churches that transition organically. This is more likely to happen in a community that consists of more second- and third-generation ethnic minorities. Sometimes there is a university nearby, where there is a diversity of people who have common interests and values. Interestingly, the first church I planted fell into this category. It was in San Antonio, a city that is wildly diverse. Given that it's in South Texas, so close to the border, there are a lot of Hispanic/Latino people who are not immigrants but whose ancestors have been in Texas for many generations and whose dominant language is English. I originally planned on the church being a Hispanic church with English- and Spanish-language elements, but I soon learned that the Lord had different plans. He added a multitude of African American, white, and Asian brothers and sisters in Christ. It truly was heaven on earth. We were so comfortable together that we could lovingly explore each other's culture. If you are someone who thinks this might be happening in your church, you are blessed! There will be a lot to learn, and some of it might happen the hard way, but help one another and extend lots of grace.

For example, I remember when the Chung family began attending my church, I hugged the husband and the wife (which I would do with everybody, as my Latino culture taught me). The daughter gasped when she saw me hug her parents. When an opportunity presented itself to gather with several Korean leaders and their families, Sister Chung pulled me aside and said, "I know at our church we hug, but when we gather with the other Korean leaders, do not hug them! Greet them from two feet away. Control yourself." I learned my lesson with lots of love! That is what I call reverse discipleship.

Sam Johnson, an African American brother, schooled me in effective preaching like no DTS professor ever did. He taught me that when you come to a rich thought, "Milk it." Say it again another way. Don't be in a hurry to move on to the next point in a message. Turn it over a few times. He lovingly critiqued the delivery of my messages, even if he enjoyed the content. He schooled me in that it is not just the content but the delivery that matters.

No matter what model you might fall into, it is vitally important to know that the process will not be easy. It will require the majority culture to give up a lot of privilege. Minority voices will need to be centered. Leaders will need to help their stakeholders, who have been raised in the homogeneous unity principle—such as elders, donors, church leaders, and influencers—to loosen the grip on their ideas and vision of church. Leaders and majority-culture members will have to begin to see values, metrics, and strategies differently. Many majority-culture members will leave, and the church may shrink before it grows. But, if it's done right, those who stick around for the long haul will eventually see the benefits, not only for them but for the community as a whole.

The Benefits of Unity through Diversity

I've already discussed how unity through diversity helps us fulfill a biblical mandate and achieve God's ultimate mission to reach all people. But there are also many other cultural benefits to multiethnic ministry that will help our church be more Kingdom oriented.

Pivoting to multicultural models will allow us the opportunity for cultural engagement that many churches have missed out on. Because of our lack of diversity, we have had ill-formed answers to the challenges of culture, and now it is smacking us in the face. We must engage the culture with more than dogma. Multiethnic unity and concern for the vulnerable can help the church walk the talk.

Diversity will help us regain credibility with younger generations. Many of us Christian leaders of a certain age have children and grandchildren who cannot reconcile their faith with a monocultural church, or a church that does not engage with the social issues of our day. Many millennials are used to living in a diverse environment because of their schools and feel uncomfortable in homogeneous environments. Generation Z is more multicultural (and multiracial) in general and doesn't know any other way.[2] They see clearly that monocultural churches do not reflect the real world. Pivoting our vision and approaches now has the potential to reengage young generations who have deemed the church to be irrelevant.

Without diversity, we live in an echo chamber of possibilities/impossibilities. Ethnic minority and immigrant leaders bring a different set of values and measures for success that help majority-culture leaders rethink our approaches. Case in point: A dear friend of mine, who is the Hispanic leader at a church in Illinois, recounted the story of when his senior pastor regretfully told him they were going to have to close the church because they didn't have enough money. The Hispanic leader said to him, "Why close the church, when we can go get jobs?" The white pastor had never considered being bivocational as a viable option. As I mentioned in a previous chapter, bivocational ministry is more common in African American and Latino churches; some leaders of color actually prefer it. Not only does it place less pressure on making money from tithes and fundraising, it also helps them make better connections in the community. This is just one example of how surrounding ourselves with different perspectives can help us to think outside of the box of the structures that white Christianity has set up for us.

Back in the day, many social programs and organizations were started by the church, but along the way much of the task has been relinquished to our government. As someone who majored in social work, I saw firsthand the benefits of government intervention in matters of the poor and marginalized; however, the delivery system tends to receive more resources than it passes on to its recipients, and it is not as effective as it was intended to be. Some of the failure of the government was because of the economy of scale. Even though our government has grown, there is no way it can keep up. Meanwhile, somewhere along the way the church became more and more inwardly focused, believing that it was relieved of its mandate to care for the poor and the marginalized. While I believe our government plays an important role in maintaining a safety net in our society, it is not our redemption and salvation. It does not absolve the church's responsibility. This is our opportunity to live out the Great Commandment while not only meeting needs but preserving dignity among all of God's people.

Transformational Communities

I've already mentioned this many times, but I'll say it again: We do not pursue diversity, multiethnic community, or a justice revival for the sake of being cool or politically correct. We should pursue them because God is calling us to it, and because this is how we will ultimately be a reconciled multiethnic community, the future of the church. I created the GC3 syllogism as a reality check and as a way of keeping us accountable. The real litmus test is community impact. We can try to pursue the Great Commission and the Great Commandment all we want, but if it's not resulting in community transformation then we are missing the point. The church needs to have a reputation in the community as the place where the people of God gather. In 2 Corinthians, Paul speaks about the church being a fragrant aroma of the victory in Christ. The church should not be a mystery to the community. The church in all its unity is supposed to make visible how God can transform a dividing wall into unity.

In chapters 4 and 6, I wrote about Shoreline Community Church in Santa Barbara, which began reaching their neighbors by starting a Spanish-language service and launching Immigrant Hope, a ministry that helps immigrants navigate the immigration process. Because they were so effectively engaging with the Great Commission and the Great Commandment together, community transformation followed. The church launched English as a Second Language (ESL) classes and driver's education classes, and out of this resulted a community education ministry, El Puente, which is shared with several churches. They began to have citywide and even regional impact. These immigrant ministries linked the church to many community agencies who began partnering with them, such as the local hospital, a diabetes clinic, the police and fire departments, and the local colleges.

The City of Santa Barbara Office of Emergency Services struggled to find and train Spanish-speaking disaster response workers. Their prior work with Immigrant Hope prompted them to partner with Immigrant Hope to pilot a first-ever Spanish-language disaster response training and team. Out of that, Shoreline Community Church became a FEMA neighborhood disaster relief site. The church's reach into the community continues to multiply. What a testimony!

Remember what I said earlier in the chapter, that multicultural ministry does not just mean ethnicity. Let me give you an example of a church in a predominantly white city that became multicultural in a different way.

Just downstream from the breathtaking Royal Gorge Bridge,

Cañon City, Colorado, straddles the Arkansas River, a tourist gateway to adventure. Tourism and a concentration of state and federal correctional facilities nearby provide modest but stable paychecks. It's a bright, shiny, family kind of place.

But hiding in the shadows, poverty, substance abuse, divorce, and homelessness lurked. Knotty Pine Motel, a rundown 1950s motor lodge known as much for sex trafficking as lodging, sat across a ditch from the Free Church of Cañon City. It was an unsightly spot that did not attract the most polished citizens. But allow me to tell you the amazing story surrounding that motel and the crazy, loving bunch at the Free Church.

One day, the Knotty Pine came up for sale. People in the community, including many at the Free Church of Cañon City, were desperate to be rid of their unsavory neighbor. But what if, one of the church's elders mused, the church could buy it? The pastor admitted that at first many thought this might be a good idea because the property was so close to them, and it might be the only way to keep a distance from their neighbors. Someone finally asked the question, What if God could use this building in a redemptive way? They began to think outside the box, and in a twist of irony, this building ended up drawing their neighbors very, very close.

After an outpouring of prayer, the church inked the ownership papers of the Knotty Pine. They asked the question, How can we get upstream and help our neighbors with long-term issues, not just quick fixes? They decided to partner with a compassion ministry called Loaves and Fishes and turn the motel into transitional housing that served the homeless in their community. The building was renamed New Creation Inn (NCI). Though it's fully operated by Loaves and Fishes, members of Free Church volunteer—serving, listening, mentoring, giving devotions, discipling, and teaching life skills. Today, the public mental health agency, the welfare department, and local substance abuse agencies partner with the church and NCI. The community notices when God is at work. A community leader was baffled, hearing that the church bought the Knotty Pine with no intention of profiting from it. "Why?" he asked. Jesus Christ, that's why. The church receives expressions of gratitude from the many community and government agencies they partner with. That blight of a motel is now a community bright spot.

And the church? There's a bridge now, literally and figuratively. They built a footbridge between the church and motel. What an apt metaphor! The people of the church have walked across the bridge into a deeper, far more relational connection with the poor and suffering. Pastor Jim Thulson has said that, every now and then, everyone on the welcome team, at the doors, and in the info center is either a current resident or an alumnus of New Creation Inn. This does not happen by design, but it is a reflection of a new reality: the poor, the marginalized, the broken, and the middle class are all family at the Free Church. Their proximity to the poor has changed them. The church is learning to love, not in theory but down in the trenches. And while doing so, they are witnessing the extension of God's Kingdom and his transforming power.

REFLECTION

Consecrating Prayer: Lord, give me a love for the beauty of the diversity of your creation. Help me work to do everything in your holy-given power to encourage it. Help me start a fire of passion for our little piece of heaven on earth in my church.

Head Work: Is your church reflecting the diversity of your neighborhood or your city? Take stock of the gap and be ready to share that with the leadership, making it clear to them that you are ready to help.

Heart Work: After reading this chapter, what makes you excited about the pivot to a multiethnic church model? What makes you nervous? What are your fears and concerns? Write them down and bring them to the Lord.

Hands Work: Come up with three next steps that you want to take on this journey. It could be reading a book on multicultural ministry, researching multiethnic churches in your city, or having a conversation with a pastor or elder at your church. We all have to start somewhere!

RESOURCES

- Study the book of Acts. Take a notebook and track the diversity developing in the book. Note the prompting of the Holy Spirit. Note the opposition.
- Book Suggestions: *Building a Healthy Multi-Ethnic Church* by Mark DeYmaz; *Multicultural Ministry Handbook* edited by David A. Anderson and Margarita Cabellon; *One Body, One Spirit: Principles of Successful Multiracial Churches* by George Yancey; *The Next Worship* by Sandra Maria Van Opstal
- The A Week in the Life series (various authors) published by InterVarsity Press is a unique resource to help you understand, through historical fiction, the challenges diversity caused in the time of the Gospels and the blessings it brought.

CHAPTER 12

Pass the Church Forward

And say to Archippus, "Take heed to the ministry which you
have received in the Lord, that you may fulfill it."

COLOSSIANS 4:17

LET'S ALL IMAGINE for a minute that we've been transported into the future. It's the year 2065. The immigrants and other marginalized people we once tried to ignore are now firmly vested in the American economic system. The population demographic shift has happened. Less than half (46 percent) of the American population is white; 95 percent of the new labor force comes from immigrants and their descendents.[1] The boomers are long gone, the Gen Xers that remain are at least eighty-five years old, and the millennials are somewhere between sixty-nine and eighty-four years old. Mainline denominations failed to maintain their doctrinal distinctives and declined.[2] The nones,[3] who in the early 2000s still believed in God/Jesus but gave up on church and left organized religion, have started their own movement that has now become its own denomination. Now here are the big questions that remain unknown: Did the evangelical church embrace the New Samaria?

Did the church experience a justice revival leading to repentance and a commitment to justice for the marginalized? Did we center immigrants and people of color, disciple them, equip them to lead, plant multiethnic churches? Do nonbelievers see the love of Jesus and unity among us?

Here is the mind-blowing reality: the answers to those questions will depend entirely on what Christians (you and me!) do now and in the next fifteen years. We cannot leave this up to chance; we must be intentional about setting ourselves up for a future church that will represent the diversity of our country and the diversity of God's Kingdom. The demographic tipping point will happen, ready or not, whether the church decides to join in or not. We must understand that our actions today, even if they are small, will impact the future tremendously. If we can grasp the magnitude of this responsibility, I believe we will be awakened from our slumbers and moved to action.

One thing I want everyone to come away with is that we were made to work together—not from positions of power or authority or superiority or political majority, but together as a church body. We must thank God for all of our differences and steward them to fulfill the mission of God. This is what will set us up for the future church.

How do we pass the church forward?

Love Being a Cultural Adventurer

When I first started working in my role, one of the first churches I visited was called First Free in Brooklyn. The church had five linguistically different congregations.

Being the cultural adventurer that I am, instead of visiting the English church, which met in the main sanctuary, I decided to go downstairs to visit the Chinese congregation, which was much larger. No, I do not speak Mandarin—remember, I am from

Laredo! I wanted to worship with saints even if I didn't speak their language. I figured the Spirit would help out: "Likewise the Spirit also helps in our weaknesses. For we do not know what we should pray for as we ought, but the Spirit Himself makes intercession for us with groanings which cannot be uttered" (Romans 8:26).

I walked in, sat in the back, and soaked in the worship. I got past the first song when a Chinese woman came up to me and said, "English service upstairs." I said, "Yes." She smiled, bowed down, and with impressive force packed in four feet, eleven inches, she said, "English service upstairs! Go now!" And I was *gone*.

Six months later I tried again. This time I was known as a national employee, and the same woman, dear Rebecca, brought an English interpreter for me. So much for Romans 8:26. After church, Rebecca offered to take my wife and me to lunch. I agreed, but only if I could pay for lunch. I thought we agreed. We went to a Chinese restaurant in Brooklyn where Rebecca ordered, in Chinese, something that was not on the menu. The food was heaven on earth. When the bill came, she grabbed it. When I reminded her of "our" agreement, Rebecca rose again in all her strength, and I was left bowing.

Get ready for changes, because according to demographic prophets, Asian immigrants will supersede Latin Americans as the largest immigrant group. Pray to God our church has embraced and empowered strong and dedicated servants of God like Rebecca!

Realize That We Have More in Common Than We Think

My perspective on love and unity changed forever the night I met Dante Upshaw. He was the director of African American ministries for my denomination. We were both to speak at a conference gathering. In order to economize on our travel budget, we decided to share a room. Our conversation that night changed my world.

It started innocuously until we shared the pain of our fathers' failures. It was like lightning hitting the sand on the beach and turning the separated parts into a chunk of glass. He, his people, his pain, his family, his future, and I, my people, my family, and my pain, were all turned into one big piece of glass.

We do not become less when we become one!

The lesson I learned with Dante is that all cultures are hurt, broken, and wounded. I learned that pain and life shared is pain lessened. I learned that I am not pained or crazy alone.

Oh, brothers and sisters, please hear me: We can realize the prayer of Jesus on earth as it is in heaven. We can have it now! We can hurt for other people so much that we feel their pain. Love, unity, and the GC3 must be lived out—every day, with every person. Think of the possibilities. Eight billion people, all made in the image of God! We must remember our mission: Make disciples of all nations.

Embrace the Fact That the New Samaria Will Make the Church Their Own

My youngest daughter, Emily, used to work in downtown San Antonio, and every day she would pass the same homeless man sleeping on the sidewalk near the door of her building. As the climate changed the man slept uncovered, and my daughter was concerned for him. One day she took a special blanket given to her by her grandmother and laid it next to the homeless man while he slept. The next day she walked by him and saw that he had ruined the precious blanket! He made a slit in it and turned it into a poncho. At first it bothered her, but as she saw how much he was utilizing it, she realized he had taken it and made it his own, and that was a good thing.

I can imagine that is the feeling the Jews had when they heard that the Gentiles had come to Christ and created their own synagogue in Antioch. Peter was dispatched to quell the plague, but when he got there he saw and felt the Spirit of God. When we entrust this special gift of God, the church, to others who are different than us, they will inevitably make it their own.

Pray to God they do, for it is they who will spread this gift to others. May they find warmth—and may they create other variations of church that resemble nothing like our church but will give them warmth and hope, and may they be a church that will live on into the future.

Keep the Main Thing the Main Thing: GC3

No matter how much you love people, love is not the objective! The objective is to point all to the Lord Jesus Christ. We were never called to build the final Kingdom here on earth. As the book of Hebrews says, "for if Joshua had given them rest, then He would not afterward have spoken of another day" (Hebrews 4:8). Instead, we are called to live like the saints exhorted to faithfulness by the examples cited in Hebrews 11: "These all died in faith, not having received the promises, but having seen them afar off were assured of them, embraced them and confessed that they were strangers and pilgrims on the earth. For those who say such things declare plainly that they seek a homeland. . . . But now they desire a better, that is, a heavenly country" (Hebrews 11:13-16).

The fact of the matter is that we can approximate the realization of the heavenly vision of heaven on earth. The full perfection of that is to come. It is in the church where that can and should come closest to being realized.

The nuts and bolts of that is in the GC3: loving people, bearing their pain as if our own; earning the right to disciple one another to become disciplemakers. The true test of our effectiveness is the community around us and whether our words match our deeds, just as the queen of Sheba saw after she tested Solomon in 1 Kings. She saw with her own eyes how his wisdom and leadership impacted his people. In the end, her testimony was the testimony we want about our church: "Happy are your men and happy are these your servants, who stand continually before you and hear your wisdom! . . . He made you king, to do justice and righteousness" (1 Kings 10:8-9).

The test is not the press clippings we glean from our own stakeholders. What does our community say about us?

Examine Your Heart

What we need to do is a bit of introspection, just as the disciples did when confronted by Jesus about long-held assumptions and sins resulting from preference, privilege, and prejudice. Maybe you deny these and say you are just being a good church person. What about the commission of God? What about the neighbor who is getting harder and harder to ignore? Here are some questions to guide us in examining our hearts:

1. Have we internalized the common cultural bias that believes and repeats the worst concerning the marginalized: they are illegal, unworthy, unreachable, beyond our cultural identity?
2. Have we pulled up the cultural drawbridge of our church, school, and home? Have we made church to meet our needs to the point that an outsider can never feel like an insider without selling his cultural soul to be part of the gang?
3. Have we reduced the message of the cross to a political litmus test such that we even wonder if people who don't vote like us are saved?
4. Have we shunned God's gift of diversity—the grain of sand that eventually yields the pearl of great price?

These questions are equally valid for those of us who are marginalized. We have made peace with the idea of all tribes not being together because we don't want to be uncomfortable. Remember the words of the woman at the well: "Why are you talking to me? Our people don't like your people" (paraphrased from John 4). Jesus did not even honor that rebuff with an answer. He was about his Father's work.

Urgency and Missional Clarity

Because of the trajectory of this country and our quickly changing demographics, we don't have a lot of time to ponder the implications of these truths for the evangelical Christian church. There is urgency in this matter. The church has lost its lamp. Many Christian leaders know this is true and have struggled to figure out how to change course. But spending more money on marketing or fine-tuning our programming is not going to solve the problem. We have focused too much on ourselves and missed the blessing of the "other." This is not about politics or economics, right or wrong. This is reality.

The question really is, Are we going to be the church that will not fail? I want the evangelical church to do what they know they are supposed to do. I want lost people to point to us and say, "Those people know God, for real!" I want people to say, "There is a God, because of the love, compassion, and integrity of those leaders." I want people to say, "That church took my side when nobody else would." I want people to say, "Those people are crazy and follow a crazy God who helps them do things that make no sense based on the culture of their day." I want people to say, "That church changed my life."

You "other" people, don't act like you are all that innocent. The disciples, with nothing, turned the world upside down. They went to their deaths as the minority, cleaned up the transgressions of the majority, stood up for the gospel, and made Christianity the world religion it is today. Paul said to submit to governing authorities, not just the ones we like. The leader at the time Paul gave this command was the evil Roman Emperor, Nero. He was the emperor who was said to be fiddling while Rome burned down. He started the fire then blamed it on the Christians. We have played the victim too long rather than following the Holy Spirit to greatness. Mind you, greatness was always in the offing. We organizational leaders have exported a Christianity that had power because of Christ but was devoid of the power of example. We have been effective because even our form of Christianity could not undo the power of God's Word.

Everybody needs to own their part in missing God's best for what this world could be. If anyone is disappointed that I have pronounced everyone as guilty, it's too late. You have made it through most of the book, and you might as well hear the rest of it out. It's too easy to go back to your corners and listen to people who will make you feel better.

Last Word Out of the Mouth of an Adventurer

Recently I was visiting Encuentro—the Spanish-speaking congregation of Northwest Community Church in San Antonio. The church was celebrating their fourth year of having a Hispanic congregation become a part of them. I wasn't planning to be there, so I felt fortunate to witness this. Pastor Dave Smith shared these thoughts (translated by pastor Manuel Abarca) in his celebration sermon at the Spanish service on Sunday:

> The first truly multiethnic church was in Antioch. From
> the names of the church leader/teachers, it is clear that
> there were rich and poor, Africans, Semites, Europeans,

and even a leader that served under Herod the king (see Acts 13:1-2).

Diversity in Antioch did not divide the church. Diversity added wrinkles and challenges that helped them consider new opportunities. No doubt their diversity helped to keep Jesus central as they sorted through cultural issues to derive the unity.

We at our own church have had many challenges—communication problems and mistakes, not taking seriously enough the uniqueness of cultures, logistics issues, and constant questioning of our biblical and cultural values. We've all had to ask for forgiveness many times. Me more than many others. We have had to learn to accommodate and offer new ways of helping people take "next steps" in becoming a disciple, other than our own typical way. Cultural diversity is a force multiplier. We have held joint worship services with both singing and sermons in English and Spanish. We have seen more and different people come to church. We have eaten more and more different kinds of food. We have made trips to Latin America and have helped start a training center in Chile. We have reached out to our community in new ways. We have hosted citizenship classes and immigration classes. We have added diversity to our elder board that helps us see ministry in new ways. In spite of challenges, I wouldn't trade the last four years for anything. We are learning the beauty of diversity. We have even explored planting other churches. Anything is possible in this church.

Pastor Dave's comment that "cultural diversity is a force multiplier" captures the essence of this book. How I long to see more pastors like Dave out there—especially in the majority culture—who see the richness in diversity, understand the importance of the GC3, and make transformation the end goal, no matter the cost.

This is my *sueño*, my dream, and I believe we can get there if we always consider ourselves students of the Master's creation, if we open our eyes to our multiethnic future and see the harvest as full, if we start living on earth as we will live in eternity.

I remember when I was leaving Laredo, standing on the porch to receive my mother's benediction. I was leaving to go to a strange world among strangers. She blessed me, then gave me the admonition to "stay away from the hippies." Peter had a similar porch scene when he was preparing to go to a new phase of his life among strangers, but the advice he received was quite the opposite. He was being sent to Caesarea, a land of Gentiles, a people hated by the Jews. Everything in his cultural psyche screamed "stay away!" but his Father told him on the porch to never call anything impure that God has made clean (see Acts 10). Love the hippies. Embrace the hippies. We're all hippies to someone.

We must bring the marginalized, the New Samaritans, from the outside into the center if we hope to pass the church forward.

Let us embrace New Samaria. Tick tock.

REFLECTION

Consecrating Prayer: Please, Lord, those words that were not of you, allow them to be forgotten. But what is of you, please sear them into our unforgettable conscience. Please use them to further awaken your church.

Head Work: Look back over the book and consider two or three points that you believe to be true but that would be sticking points for your friends. How would you say it differently in a way they would understand it?

Heart Work: Imagine what the church in your community could be like in the year 2065 if we embrace the New Samaria over the next few decades. What work do you feel God is calling you to do now in order to push the church toward that dream?

Hands Work:

1. If you are not already a committed disciple, submit to that now. It is about more than merely putting your faith in Christ alone for eternal salvation. Make a daily choice to be faithful, read his Word, spend time in prayer, be committed to fellowship with other diverse believers, and share the Good News of Jesus with others.

2. Become a disciplemaker. The highest praise to God's glory is to walk someone else through the process above and then help that person do the same for another.

3. If you are a parent, help your children walk in love through the demographic change. Find a pastor/leader of color. Pray for them and support them. It is hard but good work.

4. Be courageous as we enter into an even more multiethnic and multicultural future. Most Christians will default to the "inward church," even if they are sending millions to missions at the ends of the earth. Pray and live out the Great Commandment and the Great Commission in your backyards.

5. Finally, as this tipping point nears, fear will make all sides do hurtful things. They are the contractions of the future being birthed. Rather than being caught up in the fuss, understand the times. Let your deeds direct the birth and work to be a "beautiful church."

RESOURCES

Books for Further Study:
- *Being Latino in Christ* by Orlando Crespo
- *Brown Church* by Robert Chao Romero
- *One Blood: Parting Words to the Church on Race and Love* by John Perkins
- *Raise Your Voice* by Kathy Khang
- *Prophetic Lament* by Soong-Chan Rah
- *The Very Good Gospel* by Lisa Sharon Harper
- *Reconciliation Blues* by Edward Gilbreath
- *Intensional: Kingdom Ethnicity in a Divided World* by D. A. Horton
- *Following Jesus Without Dishonoring Your Parents* by Jeanette Yep, Peter Cha, Paul Tokunaga, Greg Jao, and Susan Cho Van Riesen
- *White Awake* by Daniel Hill
- *Leading a Healthy Multi-Ethnic Church: Seven Common Challenges and How to Overcome Them* by Mark DeYmaz

Suggested Article:
- "Re-Thinking Homogeneity: The Biblical Case for Multi-Ethnic Churches" by Aubrey Sequeira (https:// www.9marks.org/article/re-thinking-homogeneity-the -biblical-case-for-multi-ethnic-churches/)

ACKNOWLEDGMENTS

Like David's Thirty Mighty Men

THREE PHONE CALLS came in rapid succession in 2020 like the three ghosts of Scrooge, catalyzing me to begin to write this book. It had already been on my heart for twelve years.

1. Eddie Cole and Fritz Dale (work friends) told me I needed to finally write "the book."

2. Then my youngest daughter, Emily, called and asked, "Where is the book?"

3. The final kick in the pants was from a mentor and friend John Perkins. He called and asked where the book was because he wanted to write the foreword. After hearing my excuses, he said, "Hire someone to help you." Then the Lord reminded me of my dear sister Deborah Sáenz Gonzalez, who is also from Laredo and previously worked for InterVarsity Press. I asked her to be my writing collaborator, and she agreed.

Since I was already working full time, I needed someone who could help me think through and organize the vast material I had in my head, in recorded sermons, and in articles and pull it all together. Deborah was like an angel. She worked always in the background editing, rewriting, critiquing, and revising rough spots. She helped me tell the story that was within me in a way I couldn't have done on my own. (If you are in need of services like these, please, learn more about her at dsgonzalez.com.)

My friend Dennis Hesselbarth was also a big help in doing interviews and writing up the stories that were used as illustrations. Without Deborah and Dennis, this book might have sat on the shelf of memories.

I want to mention teammates: I want to thank the COSECHA team: Alex Rivero, Erik Valenzuela, Renato Jimenez, Abdel Gonzalez, Manuel Abarca, Omar Argumedo, Pablo and Xochilt Cachon, and especially Ricardo y Josephina Palmerin. I also want to thank special team members: Natalia Doriani, Karla and Barry Hannant, *y la mandona (mi mandona)* Kris Driscoll.

Friends from other cultures that have loved and instructed me include Michael and Gail Martin, April Warfield, Simon Chung, Mark Demire, Bill Sweeting, Luther Eatman, Zack Guyton, Jun Sebate, Ruth Evens, David Ruiz Molina, Rob Turner, Amy Long, Dan Reeves, Fernando and Dinorah Ronci, Javier and Belem Galindo, and many more I don't have space to name here.

Three reverse disciplers must be mentioned: Ben Johnson, David Park, and Lawrence Scott. Ben never failed to give me the "super punch" when I needed it. David is a futurist, sees the pain and failure of my generation, but hasn't given up on me . . . yet. I love you both very much. Lawrence's exhortation to be 100 percent challenged me to my core. Your best days are here and coming.

My heartfelt thanks to my prayer supporters: Tom Miller and Norman Miller of Interstate Battery System of America, Jon and Cathy Hodges, Karen Carrillo, Randy Leavitt, Charlotte Gains, Mike and Linda Grimm, Pancho and Lillie Garcia, Carlos and Angie Cuellar, and Matthew St. John.

Finally, special thanks to Dante Upshaw and Ben Johnson, two very dear and special brothers.

NOTES

INTRODUCTION

1. Bob Smietana, "Sunday Morning Segregation: Most Worshipers Feel Their Church Has Enough Diversity," *Christianity Today*, January 15, 2015, https://www.christianitytoday.com/news/2015/january/sunday -morning-segregation-most-worshipers-church-diversity.html.

2. When I use the word *evangelicals*, I am referring to Christians who believe in the Word of God and are committed to sharing the Good News of the gospel with others. It encompasses many Christian denominations. The term *evangelical* has a theological basis (literally meaning "Good News"), but it has unfortunately acquired negative connotations for some in the last few decades. Many African American and Hispanic churches identify less with the term *evangelical* and more with the terms *Christian* or *Protestant*. David Masci, Besheer Mohamed, and Gregory A. Smith, "Black Americans Are More Likely Than Overall Public to Be Christian, Protestant," *Fact Tank*, Pew Research Center, April 23, 2018, https://www.pewresearch.org/fact-tank/2018/04/23 /black-americans-are-more-likely-than-overall-public-to-be-christian -protestant/.

3. Adam McCann, "Most and Least Ethnically Diverse Cities in the U.S.," WalletHub, February 11, 2020, https://wallethub.com/edu/cities-with -the-most-and-least-ethno-racial-and-linguistic-diversity/10264/.

4. Chris Clayman, "Gateway Cities in North America," Send Institute, July 3, 2018, https://www.sendinstitute.org/identifying-global-priorities -within-north-america-for-frontier-missions/.

5. Enoch Wan proposes that the reality of demographic trends in the twenty-first century requires a three-tiered strategy: to the diaspora (evangelism and service), through the diaspora (using diaspora Christians

to reach their own), and by and beyond the diaspora (challenging diaspora Christians to engage in cross-cultural missions). Enoch Wan, *Diaspora Missiology: Theory, Methodology, and Practice* (Portland: Institute of Diaspora Studies, 2011), 185–88.

CHAPTER 1: RECALIBRATING OUR VISION

1. Charles Dickens, *A Christmas Carol* (Kathartika, 2020), 6, Kindle.
2. Dickens, *A Christmas Carol*, 50.
3. "Research and Statistics," ShortTermMissions.com, accessed October 15, 2020, https://www.shorttermmissions.com/articles/mission-trip-research.
4. "Country: United States," Joshua Project, accessed October 12, 2020, https://joshuaproject.net/countries/us.
5. James M. Kouzes and Barry Posner, *The Leadership Challenge: How to Make Extraordinary Things Happen in Organizations* (Hoboken, NJ: Wiley, 2017), 15.

CHAPTER 2: THE DEMOGRAPHIC TIPPING POINT

1. Tod E. Bolsinger, *Canoeing the Mountains* (Downers Grove, IL: InterVarsity Press, 2018), 191.
2. "Global Issues: Refugees," United Nations, accessed October 16, 2020, https://www.un.org/en/global-issues/refugees/.
3. I am only laying out the facts surrounding US immigration and the implications for us as a church. My effort is not to give any political, legal, or sociological commentary. There are many other authors who do that exceedingly well, and while I may reference some of those books later in this chapter, my goal is not to persuade you toward any political positions. I only endeavor to describe the settled reality of a major demographic paradigm shift in America.
4. Matthew Soerens and Jenny Yang's book *Welcoming the Stranger* is one of the best books about the church's response to the immigration dilemma in the US. In chapter 2, they lay out the history of immigration in the US, beginning with our country's very first settlers, through the many immigration waves of the nineteenth and twentieth centuries, leading up to today. Matthew Soerens and Jenny Yang, *Welcoming the Stranger* (Downers Grove, IL: InterVarsity Press, 2018).
5. Soerens and Yang, *Welcoming the Stranger*, 44.
6. Soerens and Yang, *Welcoming the Stranger*, 68–69.
7. "Modern Immigration Wave Brings 59 Million to U.S., Driving Population Growth and Change Through 2065," Pew Research Center, September 28, 2015, https://www.pewresearch.org/hispanic/2015/09/28

/modern-immigration-wave-brings-59-million-to-u-s-driving-population
-growth-and-change-through-2065/.

8. William H. Frey, "The Nation Is Diversifying Even Faster Than Predicted, According to New Census Data," The Brookings Institution, July 1, 2020, https://www.brookings.edu/research/new-census-data-shows-the-nation -is-diversifying-even-faster-than-predicted/.

9. "Modern Immigration Wave," Pew Research Center.

10. Isaac Mizrahi, "The Minority-Majority Shift: Two Decades That Will Chage America; Regional Shifts and Their Impact on Business," Forbes, August 25, 2020, https://www.forbes.come/sites/isaacmizrahi/2020/08 /25/the-minoity-majority-shift-two-decades-that-will-change-america -regional-population-shifts--their-impact-on-businss/?sh=352731de 590esh=.352731de580e.

11. The global population rate has reached its peak, and the world as a whole is nearing the end of a massive demographic transition. We will achieve a new balance in which population growth rate will depend less on high mortality rate (as it did in the past) and more on low fertility rates moving forward. If you look on a regional level, the other significant variable is migration. The United States is among many countries whose population growth is slightly higher *with* migration than it would be *without* migration, since there are more people arriving than are leaving. Max Roser, Hannah Ritchie, and Esteban Ortiz-Ospina, "World Population Growth," Our World in Data, 2013, https://ourworldindata. org/world-population-growth#population-growth-by-world-region.

12. "Racial/Ethnic Enrollment in Public Schools," National Center for Education Statistics, updated May 2020, https://nces.ed.gov/programs /coe/indicator_cge.asp.

13. Rob Griffin, William H. Frey, and Ruy Teixeira, "States of Change: How Demographic Change Is Transforming the Republican and Democratic Parties," The Brookings Institution, July 1, 2019, https://www.brookings. edu/research/states-of-change-2019/.

14. LifeWay Research, "Evangelical Views on Immigration," February 2015, http://lifewayresearch.com/wp-content/uploads/2015/03/Evangelical -Views-on-Immigration-Report.pdf.

15. Carey Lodge, "Evangelicals Think Immigration Threatens American Values. Here's Why They're Wrong," *Christian Today*, March 29, 2016, https://www.christiantoday.com/article/evangelicals.think.immigration .threatens.american.values.heres.why.theyre.wrong/82902.htm.

16. Thom S. Rainer, *Autopsy of a Deceased Church* (Nashville: B&H Publishing Group, 2014), 42–44.

17. M. Daniel Carroll R., *Christians at the Border* (Grand Rapids: Brazos Press, 2013), 40.
18. "Global Issues: Migration," United Nations.

CHAPTER 3: JUSTICE REVIVAL

1. Paul E. Pierson, *The Dynamics of Christian Mission: History through a Missiological Perspective* (Pasadena: William Carey International University Press, 2009), 230.
2. See Leviticus 25:8-13.
3. See Ilias Sabbir, "Theory of 'Revitalization Movement' by Anthony F. C. Wallace," https://www.academia.edu/839547/Theory_of_Revitalization_Movement_by_Anthony_F_C_Wallace, accessed January 8, 2021.
4. George Yancey, *Beyond Racial Gridlock* (Downers Grove, IL: InterVarsity Press, 2006), 21–22.
5. Hannah Furfaro, "To Understand Structural Racism, Look to Our Schools," *Seattle Times*, June 28, 2020, https://www.seattletimes.com/education-lab/to-understand-structural-racism-look-to-our-schools/.
6. Rodney Stark, *The Rise of Christianity: How the Obscure, Marginal Jesus Movement Became the Dominant Religious Force in the Western World in a Few Centuries* (Princeton, NJ: HarperCollins, 1996), 208.

CHAPTER 4: EXTENDING OUR VISION OF GOD'S KINGDOM

1. Dani McClain, "The Racial Reckoning inside Planned Parenthood," *Harper's Bazaar*, November 23, 2020, https://www.harpersbazaar.com/culture/features/a34742021/racial-reckoning-planned-parenthood/.
2. Becky Little, "Government Boarding Schools Once Separated Native American Children from Families," History, updated November 1, 2018, https://www.history.com/news/government-boarding-schools-separated-native-american-children-families.
3. National Library of Medicine, "Native Voices," National Institutes of Health, accessed November 23, 2020, https://www.nlm.nih.gov/nativevoices/timeline/543.html.
4. "U.S. Immigration before 1965," History, updated July 28, 2020, https://www.history.com/topics/immigration/u-s-immigration-before-1965.
5. Gordon Allport, *The Nature of Prejudice* (New York: Doubleday, 1954).
6. Michael O. Emerson and Christian Smith, *Divided by Faith* (New York: Oxford University Press, 2001).
7. I am not at all condoning the breaking of the law. I believe in the "rule of law," but experts on both sides of the immigration debate agree the system is broken and the issue is complicated. The point I am making is

that, while we let our government figure out this issue, we have a biblical mandate to love one another and worship together in Christ's presence, just as we will in heaven.

8. Aaron Earls, "New Hispanic Churches Often Do More with Less," Lifeway Research, July 24, 2019, https://lifewayresearch.com/2019 /07/24/new-hispanic-churches-often-do-more-with-less/.

9. Michelle Woo, "Dave Gibbons Is a Church Misfit," *OC Weekly*, September 8, 2011, https://www.ocweekly.com/dave-gibbons-is-a -church-misfit-6419157/.

10. Rick Warren, "Wilfredo De Jesús," *The 2013 Time 100*, April 18, 2013, https://time100.time.com/2013/04/18/time-100/slide/wilfredo-de-jesus/.

CHAPTER 5: APPRECIATING THE BEAUTY OF OTHER CULTURES

1. Based on phone interview with Jeff Noble on August 25, 2020.

2. "Biblical and Theological Rationale for Cultural Diversity," College of Biblical Studies, accessed October 11, 2020, https://www.cbshouston. edu/biblical-and-theological-rationale-for-cultural-diversity#_ednref5.

3. Mark DeYmaz, *Leading a Healthy Multi-Ethnic Church* (Grand Rapids: Zondervan, 2010), 45–46.

4. "San Antonio Spurs—A Win for Beautiful Basketball," The Cheap Seats, June 16, 2014, https://thecheapseats.com.au/san-antonio-spurs-a-win -for-beautiful-basketball/.

CHAPTER 6: ENTERING INTO THE PAIN OF THE MARGINALIZED

1. Tanya Basu, "How the Past 50 Years of Immigration Changed America," *Time*, September 28, 2015, https://time.com/4050914/1965 -immigration-act-pew/.

2. "Wayne Gretzky Quotes," BrainyQuote.com, accessed October 14, 2020, https://www.brainyquote.com/quotes/wayne_gretzky_131510.

CHAPTER 7: STRATEGY TRANSFORMATION

1. Jesus references the prophecy in Isaiah 61:1 (NIV), which states: "The Spirit of the Sovereign LORD is on me, because the LORD has anointed me to proclaim the good news to the poor. He has sent me to bind up the brokenhearted, to proclaim freedom for the captives and release from darkness for the prisoners."

2. "Woe to you, scribes and Pharisees, hypocrites! For you travel land and sea to win one proselyte, and when he is won, you make him twice as much a son of hell as yourselves" (Matthew 23:15).

3. Larry Osborne, *Accidental Pharisees* (Grand Rapids: Zondervan, 2012), 161. See also Tim Challies, "Gift Envy and Gift Projection," October 7, 2013, https://www.challies.com/christian-living/gift-envy-gift-projection/.

CHAPTER 8: MAKING DISCIPLES

1. Philippians 2:12 (NIV): "work out your salvation." This is not about eternal life but the walking out of that faith. It happens at different rates with different people depending on their yielding to the Spirit.
2. Steve Addison, *Movements That Change the World* (Smyrna, DE: Missional Press, 2009), 90.
3. Tony Evans and Darrell Bock, "Ethnic Identity under Christ's Authority," April 21, 2015, https://voice.dts.edu/tablepodcast/racial-reconciliation-and-church-2/.
4. Daniel Hill, "Witness or Whiteness?: Breaking Free from the Lens of White Culture in Global Mission," *Lausanne Global Analysis* 7, no. 6 (November 2018): https://www.lausanne.org/content/lga/witness-or-whiteness.
5. John C. Maxwell, *Developing the Leader within You 2.0* (New York: HarperCollins, 2018) 15.
6. Catherine Kroeger, "The Neglected History of Women in the Early Church," *Christian History* 17 (1988), https://christianhistoryinstitute.org/magazine/article/women-in-the-early-church/.
7. Robert E. Coleman, *The Master Plan of Evangelism* (Grand Rapids: Baker Publishing Group, 2010), 19–20.

CHAPTER 9: EQUIPPING LEADERS

1. Steve Addison, *Movements That Change the World* (Smyrna, DE: Missional Press, 2009), 89.
2. Bill Murphy, "China, Officially Atheist, Could Have More Christians Than the U.S. by 2030," *Houston Chronicle*, February 24, 2018, https://www.houstonchronicle.com/news/houston-texas/houston/article/China-officially-atheist-could-have-more-12633079.php.
3. Caryle Murphy, "The Most and Least Educated U.S. Religious Groups," *Fact Tank*, Pew Research Center, November 4, 2016, https://www.pewresearch.org/fact-tank/2016/11/04/the-most-and-least-educated-u-s-religious-groups/.
4. This is a generalization. There are some foreign language seminaries in the United States, but there are not many, and they are not very big.
5. Yonat Shimron, "More Seminary Students Leave the Master of Divinity Behind," Religion News Service, May 11, 2018, https://religionnews

.com/2018/05/11/more-seminary-students-leave-the-master-of-divinity
-behind/.

6. Sandra Maria Van Opstal, "Remaining to Reform," in *Still Evangelical?*,
   ed. Mark Labberton (Downers Grove, IL: InterVarsity Press, 2018), 125.
7. Shimron, "More Seminary Students."
8. Spanish slang for "guy," "dude," or "homeboy."
9. Stephen M. R. Covey, *The Speed of Trust: The One Thing That Changes
   Everything* (New York: Free Press, 2018), 1–2.
10. Earl Creps, *Off-Road Disciplines: Spiritual Adventures of Missional Leaders*
    (San Francisco: Jossey-Bass, 2006), 42.
11. Information about EFCA GATEWAY is available at the EFCA website
    (https://www.efca.org/ministries/reachnational/efca-gateway).
12. "Church Multiplication Boot Camp Curriculum" is available at the
    EFCA website (https://www.efca.org/resources/document/boot-camp
    -curriculum).
13. "Tentmaker" is a reference to any Christian who performs other jobs
    in addition to pastoral or church leadership work to provide support
    for themselves. The term comes from the Bible; it is a description of
    the apostle Paul, who supported himself by making tents while doing
    ministry in the book of Acts.
14. Rodney Stark, *The Rise of Christianity: How the Obscure, Marginal Jesus
    Movement Became the Dominant Religious Force in the Western World in a
    Few Centuries* (Princeton, NJ: HarperCollins, 1996), 174.

CHAPTER 10: ONE RECONCILED COMMUNITY

1. Tony Evans, *Oneness Embraced* (Chicago: Moody Publishers, 2015), 290,
   Kindle.
2. I call out both white people and people of color because none are
   perfect, and all have contributed to the lack of unity. This is not a time
   for pointing fingers or placing blame for our disunity. Sin and greed are
   caused by the evil of our hearts, and we are all equally capable of it.
3. Soong-Chan Rah, *The Next Evangelicalism* (Downers Grove, IL:
   InterVarsity Press, 2009), 95–98.
4. Peter Kelley, "God As a Drug: The Rise of American Megachurches,"
   UW News, August 20, 2012, https://www.washington.edu
   news/2012/08/20/god-as-a-drug-the-rise-of-american-megachurches/.
5. "What *Reveal* Reveals," *Christianity Today*, February 27, 2008, https://
   www.christianitytoday.com/ct/2008/march/11.27.html.
6. As quoted in Aubrey Sequeira, "Re-Thinking Homogeneity: The
   Biblical Case for Multi-Ethnic Churches," 9Marks, September 25, 2015,

https://www.9marks.org/article/re-thinking-homogeneity-the-biblical-case-for -multi-ethnic-churches/.

7. Adelle M. Banks, "More Multiracial Churches Led by Black, Hispanic Pastors," *Christianity Today*, January 17, 2020, https://www.christianitytoday.com/news/2020/january/more-multiracial-churches-black-hispanic-pastors-mosaix.html.

8. Christena Cleveland, *Disunity in Christ* (Downers Grove, IL: InterVarsity Press, 2013), 178–86.

9. Recipe: 1 (12 ounce) package of cranberries; 1 small garlic clove; 1 bunch green onion; 1 jalapeño pepper; 1–2 juiced limes; ½ cup sugar; 1 cup cilantro; 1½ tablespoons vegetable oil. Mix all ingredients together with a grinder or food processor. Enjoy.

10. Rodney Stark, *The Rise of Christianity: How the Obscure, Marginal Jesus Movement Became the Dominant Religious Force in the Western World in a Few Centuries* (Princeton, NJ: HarperCollins, 1996), 74.

CHAPTER 11: MULTIETHNIC MINISTRY AND TRANSFORMING COMMUNITIES

1. Mark DeYmaz, *The Coming Revolution in Church Economics*, contrib. Harry Li (Grand Rapids: Baker Books, 2019).

2. Hansi Lo Wang, "Generation Z Is the Most Racially and Ethnically Diverse Yet," NPR, November 15, 2018, https://www.npr.org/2018/11/15/668106376/generation-z-is-the-most-racially-and-ethnically-diverse-yet.

CHAPTER 12: PASS THE CHURCH FORWARD

1. "Census Bureau: 75 million more immigrants by 2060, 95% of future US growth," *Washington Examiner*, February 5, 2019 https://www.washingtonexaminer.com/washington-secrets/census-bureau -75-million-more-immigrants-by-2060-95-of-future-us-growth.

2. Some predict that mainline denominations will be gone by 2039, if the declining trend continues. See Ed Stetzer, "If It Doesn't Stem Its Decline, Mainline Protestantism Has Just 23 Easters Left," https://www.washingtonpost.com/news/acts-of-faith/wp/2017/04/28/if-it -doesnt-stem-its-decline-mainline-protestantism-has-just-23-easters-left/.

3. "Why America's 'Nones' Don't Identify with a Religion," *Fact Tank*, Pew Research Center, August 8, 2018, https://www.pewresearch.org/fact-tank/2018/08/08/why-americas-nones-dont-identify-with-a -religion/.